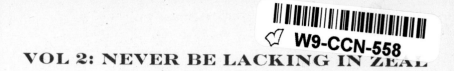

VOL 2: NEVER BE LACKING IN ZEAL

CULTURE OF REVIVAL

A REVIVALIST FIELD MANUAL

Aaron Walsh, Andrew York, Caleb Klinge
Corey Russell, David Fritch, Eric Johnson
Faytene Grassechi, Morgan Perry, Roger Joyner

Andy Byrd & Sean Feucht

Culture of Revival: A Revivalist Field Manual
Volume 2: Never Be Lacking in Zeal

Cover design by Jeremy Bardwell
at jeremybardwell.wordpress.com/bardwell-design
Interior design by David Sluka at www.hitthemarkpublishing.com

Published by Fire and Fragrance
Paperback ISBN: 978-0-9854955-2-7
Ebook ISBN: 978-0-9854955-3-4

www.fireandfragrance.com
www.thecircuitrider.com
www.burn24-7.com

Printed in the United States of America for Worldwide Distribution

Endorsements

THIS BOOK IS FILLED WITH INSIGHTS to equip the reader for a lifestyle of sustained revival. The authors are all torchbearers for this great move of God, yet their instruction is profoundly practical, paving the way for a generation to complete the mandate given by God. Read as one who has no options but to please God with every breath, and you, too, will burn with a holy fire!

Bill Johnson
Bethel Church – Redding, CA
Author, *When Heaven Invades Earth* and
Essential Guide to Healing

CULTURE OF REVIVAL IS A CRUCIAL MESSAGE to bring revelation for what a cultural reformation will look like in this current global wave of God. Sean Feucht and Andy Byrd are burgeoning young leaders, full of godly character and fresh articulation, calling a generation into abandonment and total obedience to Jesus and His teachings.

Mike Bickle
International House of Prayer – Kansas City, MO
Author, *Passion For Jesus* and *After God's Own Heart*

I LOVE THESE GUYS! My heart is so deeply moved to see this new breed of young men and women who love and honor their spiritual fathers and who carry a double portion of their love, their anointing, their vision, and their sacrifice.

When I read this book, hope erupts in me like never before with expectation for a glorious revival manifestation and an earth-shaking cultural transformation. Jesus, ruin every reader with a vision for this kind of Christianity to fill the earth!

Lou Engle
www.thecall.com

SEAN FEUCHT AND ANDY BYRD are "burning men" lighting up the nations with fire for revival. They are incredible leaders, filled with passion to see a move of God in the earth. Before we knew them personally, we saw them coming. Years ago, in the midst of a global renewal we were part of, God began to speak of an even greater revival to come—a revival in the next generation. We have prayed for years to see this generation arise. Now they are here.

In this awesome book, Sean and Andy have gathered others who are paving the way to see a "generation that will change society and society will not change them." *Culture of Revival* will show you the fire that is already burning and prepare you to become part of a generation on fire for revival.

Wesley and Stacey Campbell
www.revivalnow.com and www.beahero.org

SEAN FEUCHT IS SUCH AN EXAMPLE of a wholly-given, radical lover of God! He has a contagious passion for the Lord that draws people closer to the Father's heart and deeper into His presence. When I first encountered Fire and

Fragrance, I knew it was my tribe. Worshipping with these young people who are completely given to the Lord encouraged me into an even deeper place in God. Sean is simply a delight!

Heidi Baker, PhD
Founding Director, Iris Global

WHEN I FIRST MET SEAN AND ANDY, I was profoundly affected by their passion and purity. In the years since, I've watched their influence and impact grow exponentially. They carry a fiery, holy love across the earth, feeding the culture of that which sustains revival.

The pages of this book are incendiary and dripping with oil from the lives of some of the great, young revivalists alive today. Read it with an open heart and you just might be set on fire and launched into a life of unending love!

Charles Stock
Senior Leader, Life Center Ministries
Harrisburg, Pennsylvania

Dedication

TO THE FATHERS AND MOTHERS
who have gone before us to to pave the way for
this culture of revival to emerge. We honor the
sacrifices, obedience, and suffering you have embraced
to see God's kingdom come! You have truly taught us
to never be lacking in zeal!

Contents

Chapter 1

The Godly Virtue of Zeal

Andy Byrd & Sean Feucht

If you read *Culture of Revival: Perseverance with Joy*, we welcome you back. We pray that this book builds on the previous volume and that the culture of the kingdom becomes even more the culture of your life and community. If you are joining us for the first time, let's take a moment to reiterate the principles we are working with in the *Culture of Revival* series.

We began by calling a generation to become revolutionaries of kingdom culture. The heart of this series is to serve as an invitation to the hungry to live differently than the culture that surrounds us. We defined culture as the beliefs, shared attitudes, values, and practices that characterize individuals, families, communities, and societies. We further expanded on this definition by discussing the power of kingdom culture when the Bible defines the values and practices that we live out each day. Living out the scriptures on the earth is very much the manifestation of heaven invading earth!

Furthermore, we called each reader to become a revolutionary of culture in his or her generation. This culture, lived out by the saints, is one of the most powerful forces for change on the planet as darkness is pushed back and truth is exalted. This culture revolution is truth, empowered by the Holy Spirit, and made practical in everyday life! When this kingdom culture grips an individual, family, or a community, that entity becomes a picture of heaven on earth and the contagious nature of it is unstoppable.

In Volume 2, "Never Be Lacking in Zeal," join the quest to discover what zeal really is and how to live a life that never lacks in this essential kingdom virtue! In this day, where passivity has marked marriages, fatherhood, and much of the general spiritual climate, we must have a wake-up call! So many issues in the church, family, and society can be drawn back to lack of servant-hearted leadership, lack of initiative, passivity, and short-term passion. We must have a return to what the Bible calls zeal—a zeal that it is possible to never lack in and that compels us to a life of radical service.

We need a zeal that carries believers into their eighties and sustains moves of God more than human passion ever could. We need a zeal that is birthed, sustained, and expanded in the depths of an intimate walk with Jesus Christ! Zeal is one of the greatest virtues that we could possibly pass on to the next generation—a zeal for the lost, a zeal for God's glory, a zeal for His presence, a zeal for godly marriages and families, and a zeal for revival and reformation!

You will see from our author list that we are group of young leaders from various nations of the world. We also represent many ministries and even different streams of the body of Christ. Part of the heart and vision of this series is to model to the next generation that we can work in unity and love on the essentials for the grand purpose of the glory of God.

In each chapter, you will read personal stories and principles that have the potential and power to transform you! In addition to the authors, you will also see that we have a broad and amazing group of spiritual moms and dads who have endorsed this book. As authors, we also desire to model young leadership that is in deep relationship with the current leadership of the body of Christ and that honor this leadership. We are so privileged to have had our lives radically transformed by these mothers and fathers who have gone ahead of us!

With all of this said, let's begin! The times are pregnant with potential and harvest is upon us. We will look back in a short time and realize that we really were on the precipice of a global move of God. Revival is neither hype nor wishful thinking. Awakening is not confined to a few regions and a few streams. Global awakening is happening. Global harvest is increasing, and we have the honor of being alive in these days.

Prepare yourself in the pages ahead to be provoked and encouraged towards a lifestyle that will add fuel to the fire that is already burning around the world. Prepare to have zeal redefined, reemphasized, and made practical so that you are transformed into a zealous servant of Jesus and His ever-advancing kingdom!

Chapter 2

Radical Servant

Andy Byrd

Romans 12:11 declares, "Never be lacking in zeal." I assume the reason why you're reading this book is because you have a passion to be filled with this amazing attribute of Jesus.

However, we have to look at the rest of the verse to understand more completely what Paul meant by this phrase. Paul continued, "But keep your spiritual fervor, serving the Lord."

Serving the Lord? Yes, serving. This verse seems to infer that this is part of the very reason we are not to lack in zeal…so that we can serve the Lord with great fervor. Servanthood may not have been a topic you would have considered in a book on zeal. But let me explain further and introduce you to the greatest servant I know: my dad.

Heroes are forged in the flames of adversity. To those who overcome, a crown of beauty emerges from the ashes of disappointment and pain. My dad has always been my hero, but never so much as in the last several years.

The Pain of Loss

It had been a grueling nine months—the worst of my life. Not for one moment did I imagine that season would end the way it did. I will never forget the morning it all ended.

It was March of 2012 when I was awakened at 4:55 a.m. in a cold sweat from head to toe. It was as if the room temperature, for a moment, had risen nearly twenty degrees. I looked over at my mother sleeping in the hospital bed as I had done many times that sleepless night. Her breathing had been labored for days; she had been virtually unconscious for the last three days. All her bodily systems seemed to be winding down.

The whole family had fought for nine months against a massive boulder called "cancer." Though divine healing has always been—and will always be—a part of our life and faith, this rock never budged. Weeks of battle turned to months. Now her entrance to heaven seemed imminent.

Several days before Mom would pass away, she had met her newest granddaughter, Rhema Zoe, a name that means "a declaration of abundant life." Rhema was a glimmer of hope and life to Mom as she valiantly fought for her own survival. When my wife and children had arrived in Alaska where Mom and Dad were living, we had placed Rhema on Mom to introduce her for the first time. Rhema was six months old. My mom strained to open her eyes. She could utter no words, but she was able to eek out a smile. It would be her last smile and the last time we would see her beautiful blue eyes.

Anticipating that her final night had come, my brother and I decided to sleep on the couches in our living room to be with her. Several times that night I had woken to see if she were still breathing—to see if the strained veins on her chest were still pumping blood.

This particular time I looked over and saw what I thought to be a breath. I kept watching just to double check. It was in that moment that my mom was ushered into heavenly glory. I had seen her last breath, her last heart beat. I can't explain that moment. Words do no justice to my emotions, though most people may understand from their own losses in life. She was only fifty-eight years old. I was only twenty-nine. I sat up on the couch realizing what had just happened, woke my brother up and, through prayer, put a stake in the ground.

"God, we don't understand, but we don't have to," we prayed. "If we want the peace, we must be willing at times to give up the understanding. We refuse to believe that You are anything but good! We will never again have the opportunity to worship in this situation, so we choose to exalt you."

True Family

As I have reflected on this occasion these last several years, I have seen nothing but amazing redemption come out of this loss. This chapter is about one of those primary redemptions in the midst of such pain and loss.

My parents always had a great marriage. I am one person, of all too few, who saw Jesus in their parents' lives and marriage. I never had a reason to doubt anything but God's goodness.

My mom and dad were great friends and amazing parents. Our family had spent the early years creating a community out in the woods of northeastern Washington State. Our dream was to live the Bible on a daily basis.

It was an amazing way to start my life. We were totally dirt-poor in terms of money and yet rich in family love, deep devotion to God and His word, and a community as close to heaven as I could imagine. From this little hamlet in the woods, we made the bold, and somewhat odd, move to Adak Island in the remote Aleutian Islands of Alaska. During the next four years, we lived in a beauty few will ever get to enjoy. Winds up to one hundred miles per hour, one sunny day a month, not a single freestanding tree on the island, and all the adventures a young boy could ever want, awaited us.

Mom and Dad continued to do their best to lead us into a love for each other, for God, and a desire to make a difference no matter where we lived. Those four years were bliss for my biologist dad, survival for my Southern Californian mom, and non-stop adventure for my brother and me.

After these four years, our family made another move to Homer, Alaska. At least Homer was connected by road to the rest of civilization. It was a big move for the family and largely done out of Dad's heart to honor Mom's desire to be closer than a four-hour flight from the nearest town. All through this time, our greatest strength was the bond of our family. A loving mom and dad along with friendship and surrender to Christ were at the center of it all. I feel so blessed to have this testimony and this upbringing.

From Devoted Husband to Radical Servant

The remainder of my junior high and high school years were spent in Homer. Before long, I was off on my own, working with Youth With A Mission and traveling around the world. It was twelve years later I received a phone call from Mom with the news of her cancer diagnosis. From the first call, our whole family entered into an all-out war for her life. Prayer, fasting, and medical care were kicked into high gear as we, and hundreds of others, rallied for my mom's breakthrough over this life-threatening disease.

But it was not long before the cancer had spread throughout her body. The doctor said it was the fastest growing cancer he had ever seen. Due to the extensive tumors in her body and the chemotherapy, Mom quickly became completely dependent on help for moving, sleeping, using the bathroom, and every area of life. In the nine months that would follow, I saw in my dad the clearest picture of Christ I have ever seen in a person. It was as if Jesus had taken on human skin in the form of my dad, and through this I learned perhaps one of the greatest lessons in my life.

We Most Serve That Which We Most Cherish

I would say that Dad was an amazing husband to Mom. My dad would say he never learned to truly cherish his wife until she was in the grip of a disease that would take her life. In that moment, his deep love for biology and nature took the back seat as he stopped everything to wait on Mom and her every need.

I watched Dad rise up as a warrior in intercession as if his words were the very swords that could push back the disease and its demonic roots. I watched him become the most tenderhearted man I had ever seen as he waited on Mom's needs. I watched him sitting at her side as she wasted away, reading her the Psalms and singing the hymns they had sung since their youth. I watched as he checked her into the hospital again and again as complications to her treatments threatened to take her life even before cancer did.

He was never far from her side for nine months. She was never far from his mind for those months. All of his desires were easily passed over in hope that he might not lose his wife. Somehow, even in that loss, a major victory was won. Today he would say he did not know what it really meant to cherish someone until the potential for losing her entered his mind.

Out of that profound and mysterious love, perhaps the strongest force on the planet, a hard-working and devoted husband became a radical servant to the very point of laying down his life. If he could have somehow given his life that she would have been spared, he would have done so in a moment. We don't know how much can be given up until we are stretched beyond all selfish ambition, personal gain, and self-service by the desperate need of those that we most love. My dad's devotion to my mom turned into a profound love that was defined by a radical willingness to sacrifice all for her and to serve her tirelessly. This is a hero. This is a leader.

Cherish and We Will Serve

The principle I saw Dad exemplifying was that people only truly serve what they truly cherish. Perhaps the lack of servant-hearted leadership that our culture experiences today actually stems from the fact that those in leadership do not cherish the people around them. Our issue may be more a deficiency of the love described in 1 Corinthians 13 than a lack of revelation of the importance of serving.

Losing Mom changed many things in my life and family; yet, one of the most startling and life-changing revelations for me was the question of whether I have ever truly learned to cherish and love others as Christ loves the bride. Can I really look at my four beautiful children and my wife of twelve years in the face and be confident that I have not just served them out of religious routine and obligation?

The sure sign of this lack of love is how easily and quickly I hit the ceiling of my willingness to serve and revert back to self-focus and selfishness. Can I view the lost, hurting, dying world around me and cherish them as Christ did? Does my heart overflow with the love I watched ooze out of Dad as he labored on behalf of Mom month after month?

It is possible to have a type of serving without cherishing. It can look good in public, especially when others are watching.

But when we learn to cherish, it becomes virtually impossible to not enter into radical servanthood. We will naturally and un-apologetically serve that which we most cherish. This says a lot about what we actually cherish. Our willingness to fight for our own rights, comforts, and ways is a very clear indicator of the level of self-cherishing that goes on in society. We are in love with our desires and ourselves to such a degree that we will break relationships to get our own way.

Why are customer service desks the least-desired jobs in a store? Is it because customers really cherish themselves? Numerous times I have found myself embarrassed at the way people will treat flight attendant or a ticket agent at the airport. We really cherish our aisle seats and on-time schedule more than we do the human standing in front of us.

Often we hear waitresses confess that the worst day to work at a restaurant is Sunday. "Sunday customers are the rudest, pickiest, and least generous people I serve on a weekly basis," they will say.

We really cherish our food the way we want it. "Mustard is unacceptable! I want a new burger! Yes, throw the other one away!"

How will we feel in the halls of eternity when we look back on having cherished a hamburger without mustard more than the human who was serving it to us? This may be an appropriate time to stop reading right now and repent for the lack of love in our hearts for those around us.

Jesus never encountered a person that He did not love perfectly. He *never* put His own desires and wishes above cherishing the eternal being that stood in front of Him. If anyone had the right to a burger without mustard, it was Jesus. Yet, time and again, He put the needs of others above His own comforts and desires. Had He not, we would have no salvation. Yet, we have taken that free gift of salvation and turned it for personal gain and peace without fully embracing the very culture and character of the man who gave it to us.

Imagine the power of a church revived in servanthood. It would look, smell, and act like Jesus. Jesus is very clear on the point. He makes dozens of references to a servant in the Gospels, while He only mentions leadership twice (both times in the context of servanthood).

Why are there so many books on leadership and so few books on radical serving? It's because serving doesn't sell books. Leadership evokes feelings of influence, title, and position. Serving produces fear that we will never be noticed or have our moment of fame. Who wants to buy a book on how to not be first, noticed, encouraged, patted on the back, sat in the middle of a room and affirmed, clapped for, or even have a known name? All the while, Jesus sits in the shadows, the lone author of true servanthood, looking for those who will carry His DNA. Oh, that others would join Him in His efforts to create true leaders with heaven's paradigm and perspective. As we examine what Jesus calls servanthood, let us also identify and destroy false forms of servanthood so that we might more fully recognize and live in the genuine.

The Selective Servant

Consider the "Selective Servant": the first one to volunteer when serving actually gains attention. The selective servants do not actually cherish those they are serving but rather cherish the acknowledgement of public serving! Oh, it should not be!

> "Be careful not to practice your righteousness in front
> of others to be seen by them. If you do, you will have
> no rewards from your Father in heaven."
> —Matthew 6:1, NIV

In the same context of secret generosity, prayer, and fasting comes Jesus' command to store up treasures in heaven rather than on earth. Could it be that true, radical servant-hearted living reaps some of the greatest heavenly rewards? Could it be that my dad's greatest accomplishment in sixty-five years of life was to love my dying mom as Christ loved the church, even as cancer stole her dignity and beauty? Few human eyes saw what my dad went through--the tears, prayers, and cherishing that took place. Could it be that heaven looked on with amazement and awe at my dad and saw a man who was acting as his Savior did? The scriptures exalt a man who is willing to become a hidden slave of all. Jesus said,

> "And whoever wants to be first must be your slave--
> just as the Son of Man did not come to be served, but
> to serve and to give his life as a ransom for many."
> —Matthew 20:27–28, NIV

Let us consider the parable of Luke 17. On the heels of learning to forgive, and faith for the impossible, Jesus tells us a story about true servanthood and what it should look like:

"Suppose one of you has a servant plowing or looking after the sheep. Will he say to the servant when he comes in from the field, 'Come along now and sit down to eat?' Won't he rather say, 'Prepare my supper, get yourself ready and wait on me while I eat and drink; after that you may eat and drink?' Will he thank the servant because he did what he was told to do? So you also, when you have done everything you were told to do, should say 'We are unworthy servants; we have only done our duty.'" —Luke 17:7–10, NIV

Serving is an honor and a privilege to be highly esteemed in our hearts--but not for the acclaim and attention of others. It is not a "cherry-on-top" to serve or even a great "above-and-beyond" action. *To be a Christian is to be a servant.* God wants to give us a paradigm shift on serving so we do not see it as a favor we are giving, but a grace we are granted. The honor is ours to serve! Gratitude is not the goal; attention is not the goal. Serving is an end as much as being "like Christ" is an end.

The Somber Servant

Then there is the "Somber Servant" similar to the character Eeyore in *Winnie-the-Pooh*. He is willing to help, even volunteering perhaps, but no smile shall cross his face. Deep sighs replace normal breathing.

Spare us the self-pity speech. Spare us the labored lifting of feet to do the very thing that ought to be an outright eternal honor. Imagine Jesus sighing with frustration as He labored on the cross.

"Oh, Father, is this finally enough?" "Did You see how much that hurt?" "I think I need a vacation, a sabbatical perhaps!" "I need a season of no responsibility, I am burnt out."

Let us not think that burnout is just the result of over-serving. Instead, lack of intimacy is often the true cause of our burnout. As Jesus peered at the hill of suffering that awaited Him, He measured the pain, checked in one more time with the Father, and then "for the joy set before Him" forever set the benchmark of true leadership. He did what no one could do for themselves, and He did it motivated by love and cherish for those He served.

With every act of joy-filled serving here on earth, an eternal boatload of rewards is stored up. The first on earth are often the last in heaven, and the last on earth are the first in heaven (Matthew 19:28–30, NIV). Usually, the Somber Servants are looking more for a word of affirmation than the satisfaction of emulating and honoring Christ and cherishing those around them. Their motivation is: "If I sigh loud enough, someone will ask me how I am doing which is really what I want: someone to hear how hard my life is and feel as badly for me as I feel for myself."

The Self-Serving Servant

We can't move on without a diagnosis of the "Self-Serving Servant." This close cousin of the Selective Servant actually seeks to serve only within the boundaries of personal comfort. This type of servant is more interested in personal entertainment, satisfaction, and personal agendas than in walking in Christ-like servanthood. The travesty of this paradigm is that though heaven may be their eternal home they will for all of eternity live with the reality that they cared more about hanging on to comfort, agenda, personal offenses, and entertainment than personally sacrificing and joyfully serving the world around them.

How will the joy of heaven and the regrets of earth coexist? Only God knows. But I assure you, in the end, we would rather joyfully serve unto our dying breath than enter eternity with our eyes fixed on ourselves. For some, gazing upon the Eternal Judge will be the first time they have practically looked at anyone but themselves. Let it not be so! Let it not be true of us!

Keep Your Spiritual Fervor Serving the Lord

I've already quoted Paul's command to the church from Romans 12:11, "Never be lacking in zeal. But keep your spiritual fervor, serving the Lord."

Could it be that zeal and spiritual fervor are directly connected to serving the Lord and *for* the sake of serving the Lord? What is all our zeal for, if not to become greater servants of the Lord? What good is spiritual fervor—which means to boil over with passion—if it does not lead us to a more sincere and wholehearted devotion to serving the Lord's every desire? The word *serve* here is from the Greek root word *doulos*, which is the term for a bondservant or slave: one who has committed themselves to their master for life, but is based in a revelation of mutual love. The usage of the word "Lord" at the end of the verse is also appropriate as it declares the idea of a master with authority.

So the verse could be read like this: Never be lacking (don't be shrinking back, lazy, idle, or timid) in zeal (diligence) but keep your spiritual fervor (hot, boiling over) serving (as a bond slave) the master (who has all authority and superiority).

Jesus, the Ultimate Example

The life, teaching, and sacrifice of Jesus began to make so much more sense to me through the loss of my mom. The greatest redemption that came from losing Mom was that I experienced

a revelation into an area of Jesus's heart that I had never known
before. If Dad could cherish and sacrifice so much, what emotion filled the heart of Jesus that He would give up everything
and lay His very life down to serve and save a people who were
guilty of the death penalty? What did Jesus understand about the
kingdom and true love that we do not? Why would He so emphasize the servant role throughout Scripture? Not many topics are
addressed in the Bible more than servanthood, including leadership, marriage, and parenting—probably because the teaching on
servanthood is the revelation of being a godly leader, spouse, and
parent. Many of us do not yet understand that servanthood is so
much more than simply performing a few menial tasks.

Jesus, the ultimate servant, was motivated by an intense devotion to the human race. This intensity served as the furnace of
love that would take an innocent man to the cross to win freedom
for a guilty people.

In our modern time, it seems that leaders have become celeb-
rities: isolated from the average person, and untouchable to many
that they lead. This is so far from the model of Jesus as a radical
servant that it hardly resembles true Biblical leadership at all. In
fact, Jesus only mentions the word *leadership* a handful of times
in the Gospels and it is *always* in reference to leadership as being
the servant of all.

He said,

> "But among you it will be different. Whoever wants
> to be a leader among you must be your servant, and
> whoever wants to be first among you must be the
> slave of everyone else." —Mark 10:43, NLT

"The greatest among you must be a servant."

—Matthew 23:11, NLT

"But among you it will be different. Those who are the greatest among you should take the lowest rank, and the leader should be like a servant."

—Luke 22:26, NLT

The late missionary and radical servant of Jesus, Jim Elliot, said that there is not one word in the New Testament about training for leadership—all the training is for being a servant. Where is this understanding and desire in the church today? How often is someone heard praying in great joy and faith, "Make me a servant like Jesus," or "Show me how to see myself as the lowest rank." Yet again and again this is what Jesus not only modeled, but also taught as the way of the kingdom. It is truly an upside-down kingdom.

Too often we have bought into a corporate idea that someone who may have a leadership role, title, position, influence, or even finances, is to be treated as a higher life form. The idea is propagated by society but is also easily fallen into by leaders themselves. Jesus treated every human with the same dignity. He served all, no matter their position in life. Everyone wants to add their titles to their name cards, websites, and email footers. What would Jesus' name card have said? "Servant of all," "Dying that others might live," "Homeless, jobless, and poor," "Beloved Son of God," "Despised and rejected by all," "Loved by the uncreated God."

Zealous Serving

Let none despair, and allow no condemnation to drive us to serve. Rather, let us take up the great challenge and joy of being like Christ in all things. Think of the reward for the radical servant. Think of the lives changed by the ones who are wiling to be last. Oh, the very aroma of Christ cannot be quenched as believers joyfully and zealously bow low to elevate Christ and others. Could this be the key to the joy we look for in so many other things? Imagine the Bride as the ultimate servant of all of mankind: a bride like Mary who was found willing to do anything the angel of the Lord said to her. This type of radical servant can carry the most world-shaking promises of God.

Now is not the hour of discouragement or resolving in our minds that we may never be a servant like Jesus. Today is a day to shatter self-preoccupation and take on selfless focus that is enamored with Jesus so that we can joyfully lay our lives down to serve His purposes in our generation! Biblical heroes and all great men and women of history cheer us on with the testimonies of their lives and the impact of those who, out of deep love for God and others, made an undeniable impact for the kingdom!

Zealous Cherishing

I remember Mom telling me just before she died that even in the midst of a horrific disease, she was so grateful for the nine months of deep cherishing and servant-hearted love that she and my dad were able to share. She died knowing more than ever that she was loved.

My dad is a hero of sincere love and servanthood. He has become a voice—to me and all who know him—of the power of cherishing and serving. He has determined in his heart that to live like Christ is to cherish and serve like Christ—until we see Him face-to-face! Will you take up this same challenge?

Then he said, "Do you understand what I have done to you? You address me as 'Teacher' and 'Master,' and rightly so. That is what I am. So if I, the Master and Teacher, washed your feet, you must now wash each other's feet. I've laid down a pattern for you. What I've done, you do. I'm only pointing out the obvious. A servant is not ranked above his master; an employee doesn't give orders to the employer. If you understand what I'm telling you, act like it—and live a blessed life." —John 13:12–17, MSG

About the Author

Andy Byrd and his wife, Holly, have dedicated their lives to spiritual awakening in a generation and in the nations. They work with a group of life-long friends committed to consecrated community, Christ-centered living, revival, and cultural reformation. They are part of the leadership of University of the Nations, YWAM Kona, and have been with YWAM since 1998, traveling to many different nations with a heart to help raise up a revival generation to live in the confluence of prayer/intercession and gospel/mission. Andy and Holly have helped give birth to Fire and Fragrance ministries and the School of the Circuit Rider. One of the greatest delights of their lives and primary area of focus is their four children Asher, Hadassah, Rhema, and Valor. Contact Andy at www.andybyrd.com, www.fireandfragrance.com, or www.thecircuitrider.com.

Chapter 3

Cultivating a Dreaming Heart

David Fritch

Several years ago on a ministry trip to Arkansas, I met a ten-year-old girl whose simple, faith-filled words shifted the entire direction of my life. One night after dinner, I asked her what she wanted to do when she grew up. She said, "I want to be a hairstylist, end child slavery, and start orphanages all over the world." I was amused she had so casually put being a hairstylist in the same category with such heroic acts of justice. But I was more so in awe of her simple faith that her dream could actually happen.

For the next few days, I could not stop thinking about my conversation with this little girl. God was using it to show me the stark contrast between my heart and hers. I realized I had lost this child-like optimism and had stopped dreaming. From this mo-

ment on, God took me on a journey—showing me a trail of ap-
pointments, shattered illusions, and hurt that led me to this point.

During this season, God highlighted Proverbs 13:12, which
says, "Hope deferred makes the heart sick, but desire fulfilled is
a tree of life" (NASB). I saw that God wanted to use this verse to
begin the process of healing my heart and teaching me how to
dream again. I want to share with you the priceless truths God
taught me through this powerful verse. My prayer is that something deep inside of you will be awakened and you will begin to
dream God-sized dreams that have the potential to rewrite the
destiny of cities and nations.

Created to Dream

We were created to dream. When we dream, we reflect the image of our all-powerful and unlimited Father. Dreaming involves
the imagination, which is the realm that is the most like God. In
the imagination there are absolutely no limitations of time, space,
or ability. It is the place where the impossible becomes possible.
We see this incredibly demonstrated when children play. On one
day, they can be flying superheroes that shoot lasers from their
eyes and save the world, and on another day they can go back in
time and slay dragons with the Knights of the Round Table.

A dream is when God paints a picture on the canvas of our
imagination, showing us what He wants the future to look like.
In a sense, dreaming allows us to pull the future into the present moment, observe it with our inward eye and then begin the
task of building what we see. These powerful visions will cause
us to emerge from the slavery of earthly limitations and step into
the unlimited power of the Holy Spirit. Then we will witness the
greatest overthrow of darkness we have ever seen.

ment on, God took me on a journey—showing me a trail of disappointments, shattered illusions, and hurt that led me to this point.

During this season, God highlighted Proverbs 13:12, which says, "Hope deferred makes the heart sick, but desire fulfilled is a tree of life" (NASB). I saw that God wanted to use this verse to begin the process of healing my heart and teaching me how to dream again. I want to share with you the priceless truths God taught me through this powerful verse. My prayer is that something deep inside of you will be awakened and you will begin to dream God-sized dreams that have the potential to rewrite the destiny of cities and nations.

Created to Dream

We were created to dream. When we dream, we reflect the image of our all-powerful and unlimited Father. Dreaming involves the imagination, which is the realm that is the most like God. In the imagination there are absolutely no limitations of time, space, or ability. It is the place where the impossible becomes possible. We see this incredibly demonstrated when children play. On one day, they can be flying superheroes that shoot lasers from their eyes and save the world, and on another day they can go back in time and slay dragons with the Knights of the Round Table.

A dream is when God paints a picture on the canvas of our imagination, showing us what He wants the future to look like. In a sense, dreaming allows us to pull the future into the present moment, observe it with our inward eye and then begin the task of building what we see. These powerful visions will cause us to emerge from the slavery of earthly limitations and step into the unlimited power of the Holy Spirit. Then we will witness the greatest overthrow of darkness we have ever seen.

History Was Written by Dreamers

History was written by dreamers. Every great movement, successful business, and justice initiative was catalyzed by ordinary people provoked by an awe-inspiring picture of the future. Where would our generation be without men like the Wright brothers, Albert Einstein, and Martin Luther King Jr.? These men practiced the art of dreaming, which is to look beyond what the world is in order to see what it could be. Dreamers see what others cannot see and therefore do what others will not do.

It's amazing to think that the great nation of America emerged from a single, solitary idea in the hearts of men who made incredible sacrifices to make their vision a reality. I often wonder if these men imagined that future generations would live out their dream, establish a culture of freedom, and give rise to some of the greatest breakthroughs in science, technology and medicine in modern history.

What are we handing off to the next generation? Is it possible that the next generation could never know the apathy, indifference, and barrenness of the church of today? Could it be possible that the children of today grow up to become the adults who know a world where abortion is abolished, sex trafficking has ended, and the pornography industry is bankrupted? Could it be possible that in twenty years AIDS and cancer are only distant memories and stories we tell our children? Could it be possible that we could receive a revelation from heaven so big that it ignites revival movements in cities, campuses, and churches that sweep millions into the kingdom of God?

It blows my mind to think that what a sixteen-year old writes in his journal today could alter the course of nations tomorrow. The earth is groaning and waiting for sons of the most-high God to step into the fullness of who they are. To not discover, cultivate, and act on your dreams is to rob the next generation of break-through. What are you dreaming about?

Dreaming Energizes Us

When a dream is from heaven it has incredible power on it. It carries the ability to energize us and to sustain us when we face resistance. Let me give you an example. Recently, God placed a dream in my heart to write a book. As I faced-off with the dread-ed blank page, I was assailed by all the mental enemies that rein-forced what I was already feeling inside: "You can't write; you'll never write anything good." As I was sparring with these emo-tional bullies, a friend of mine called and, without any knowledge of the battle I was in, began to encourage and prophesy to me about writing.

His prophecy helped me get in touch with the dream I had in my heart. He reminded me of the call, the passion, and the desire that had been beaten down by discouragement. As soon as I hung up the phone, this incredible energy rose up in me, and I wrote for the rest of the day. Zeal and passion are the by-products of a God-breathed dream. A dream from God will not only motivate us to start well, but will also inspire the kind of discipline neces-sary to finish well.

Dreaming Fosters Discipline

The only thing that will stop us from actually turning our dreams into reality is not exercising the discipline necessary to put them into action. Self-discipline is what separates day-dream-ers from world changers. Discipline is vital to greatness; yet, we will never find the strength of heart to endure the pain of disci-pline without a powerful, God-inspired dream. As Danny Silk, a senior leader at Bethel Church in Redding, California, says in his teaching series called *Dream Life*, "Dreams give pain a purpose."[1]

A vision from heaven becomes a source of motivation that gives our life focus and helps us decide when we should say yes and when we should say no. King Solomon put it this way, "Where there is no vision, the people are unrestrained" (Proverbs 29:18, NASB). In other words, he was saying that when we receive a mandate from heaven, it causes us to restrain our options in order to fulfill it.

Dreaming Is the Doorway to the Supernatural

At the end of the day, we must understand that self-discipline alone cannot help us fulfill our dreams. A God-inspired vision will always be bigger than our ability to achieve in our own human strength. A dream provokes humility; it beckons us out of the status quo and into the supernatural realm where we co-labor with God to do extraordinary exploits.

We weren't meant to be orphans trying to figure out life and pursue our dreams on our own. We have a Father that is committed to doing life with us. He designed us to be partners with Him in the family business and has made the resources of heaven available to us to fulfill our mission. Just think; we have access to the knowledge, wisdom, power, and wealth of an unlimited Father. We have been set up to succeed.

The Life Cycle of a Dream

Solomon said, "Desire fulfilled is a tree of life" (Proverbs 13:12, NASB). The tree is a picture of the believer whose desires have matured into a lifestyle that impacts the world in powerful ways. The tree gives us great insight into the lifecycle of a dream. A dream starts as a seed, which is an idea or desire planted in our hearts by the Holy Spirit. Our dreams are not mere products of human desire, strategic planning, or good brainstorming, but they have their origin in God and come as we abide in His presence. The Apostle John put it this way, "He who abides in me and I in him, he bears much fruit" (John 15:5, NASB).

A prophet once said to me, "David, why did God create you?" Of course, I had some theologically sound, well thought-out answers in mind like, "I was created to worship," or "I was created to take the gospel to the ends of the earth." But before I could give any of my great answers she said, "God didn't create you to do anything for Him; He simply created you to be the recipient of His overflowing love." This truth delivers us from the idea that the sole existence of our life is merely to produce something. It releases us into a place of rest and security where we can begin to live from a place of overflowing love.

There is a lot of talk these days about revival and reformation. These are noble and godly pursuits; however, if these things drive us more than the presence of God, we will have tragically missed the point. The primary ingredient to a culture of revival is the passionate pursuit of His presence. This pursuit must come above all other things, including the quest to have a high-impact ministry. Jesus is revival and when we get Him, we get everything.

God always prioritizes intimacy above productivity. We cannot help but bear fruit when we align ourselves with heaven's priority and find a place of intimate friendship with God. As we pursue intimate friendship with the Lord, passionate godly desires will burst forth from our hearts and dreams will be born that change the world. These desires are a product of our new life in Christ and are roadmaps of our destiny. If we are pursuing the Lord as the prize of our lives, we shouldn't be suspicious of these desires when they spring up. We should especially pay attention to the thoughts and desires that emerge when we are in the presence of God.

The Way of Death

Dreams are born when God breathes on our hearts in the place of intimacy. However, if we do not understand the journey of a dream as a seed to a tree of life, we may get disheartened and stop pursuing them. The reality is that if we were to step into the fullness of God's plan for our life all at once, it would crush us. God mercifully takes us through a maturing process so that we will develop the kind of character necessary to fulfill our dreams.

In our well-meaning, motivational speeches on changing the world, we fail to tell young people that they will have to go the way of death to fulfill their destiny. The apostle John wrote, "Unless a grain of wheat falls into the earth and dies, it remains alone" (John 12:24, NASB). This process is both painful and necessary. This is a season where God does a work at a deep level in our hearts and exposes the attitudes and mindsets that are not in alignment with who He is. This phase of life is called the wilderness.

The wilderness is a place of silence, waiting, and sometimes-unanswered prayer. During this time, our hearts are purified of pride and selfish ambition, and everything we have trusted in, other than God, is challenged. Just as Jesus was tempted in the wilderness before He emerged to shift the course of human history, we will also be tested before we fulfill our calling. The wilderness is a place where the most important battles for our heart are fought. These battles are about how you view God and how you see yourself.

Will we still trust Him and believe He is good in the midst of hardship, even when things don't work out as we hoped? When people fail us and our prayers go unanswered? It's during these times of waiting that the enemy tempts us to choose self-pity over perseverance, despair over hope, and accusation over trusting God. This is a time when many partner with the enemy's lies, develop a sick heart, and stop dreaming. However, if we trust the Holy Spirit to complete His work in us, our tribulation will "bring about perseverance; and perseverance, proven character; and proven character hope; and hope does not disappoint" (Romans 5:5, NASB).

Getting a Sick Heart

Proverbs 13:12 says, "Hope deferred makes the heart sick" (NASB). Many have set out with fiery zeal to do great things for God only to face the brutal reality of spiritual resistance, inner emotional battles, personal weakness, failure, disappointment, and unanswered prayers. If we face enough "hope deferred," our hearts will eventually become sick.

The key characteristic of a sick heart is hopelessness. Hopelessness comes with a pack of lies such as: "There are no options," "You are a victim," "Failure is what you can expect from life," "God is not for you," and "You can never change."

To choose hopelessness is to choose life under the ceiling of Satan's lies. This hopelessness encourages us to be comfortable with a mediocre, low-impact existence. When our hearts are sick, we lose the ability to dream and as a result we slip into survival mode where we never expect too little or too much from life. In this frame of mind, routines become a false source of comfort to us because of the predictability and sense of security they provide. I believe heaven weeps when the sons of God forget who they are and stop dreaming. Have you stopped dreaming, and, if so, why?

Here are a few symptoms that might help you understand if you have a sick heart.

- You've stopped dreaming.
- All of your dreams are attainable with your strengths and abilities.
- You've stopped asking for prayer.
- You experience loss of creativity.
- You have loss of motivation.
- You've stopped asking, "What if?"
- You struggle with depression or despair.
- You are cynical (you see the bad and expect the worst).
- Your routines have become a false comfort.
- Life happens to you rather than you happening to life.
- You don't believe you can change.
- You are angry at God.
- You stop making plans for the future.

God is committed to healing our hearts and restoring us from the disappointments and the failures of life. You must recognize that there is an enemy of your soul that does not want you to see your potential in God or to fulfill your dreams. It seems that Satan sends a million messages a day, which are meant to discourage you or to blur your vision of the goodness of God. But if we trust the Holy Spirit to complete His work in us, then we will emerge with strong, unwavering hope.

Hope is our destination. God created us to live in an atmosphere of hope. The message of faith has been proclaimed far and wide in the last few years, but very rarely do we hear about the importance and role of hope. Faith is the firm conviction of God's ability to act on our behalf, but hope is the eager expectation that

He is going to do it for us and that it could happen at any moment. Hope is the sustaining force that helps us weather every season of the soul until our lives become a tree of life and we fulfill every dream He has birthed in us. Dreams are seeded in intimacy, tested in the wilderness, and sustained through hope.

Healing the Sick Heart

Chances are you didn't get a sick heart overnight; rather, you acquired it through a variety of difficult experiences. Healing is the process where God exposes Satan's lies and transforms our minds, both about how we view God and how we view ourselves. Healing is a deeply personal and relational journey we must choose to walk through with the Lord. The following are few ways God has helped me find healing.

1. **Get real with God**. This is where true freedom begins. Many people become experts at avoiding the pain in their hearts by living noisy, busy, and overindulgent lifestyles. If you choose to stuff, numb, or avoid your pain, it will most likely manifest as anxiety, depression, mood-swings, and even rage. The price we pay in our personal relationships when we choose not to deal with our hearts can be devastating.

We must find a place to express our hearts to the Lord. The prophet Isaiah encourages us that God will comfort all who mourn in Zion (Isaiah 61:2-3). Zion symbolizes the presence of God. The prophet was saying that the presence of God is the best place to pour out our pain because it's there we will receive everything we need. Abba Father loves it when we vent our emotions in His presence. He can take it. In fact, He already knows the depth of our emotion, and He also knows the sweet release that comes as we open our hearts to Him.

2. Forgive those who hurt or disappointed you. Much of the pain we have stored up in our hearts has been inflicted on us by other people. When we choose to forgive those who have hurt us, it liberates us from the emotional ties to that person and positions us to receive healing for all the associated memories. When we choose to give mercy where judgment is deserved, we model the unconditional love that was given to us by our heavenly Father. When we ask the Father for grace to forgive, He will be faithful to provide it. Forgiveness is a journey of the heart; it takes time and cannot be produced on demand. It happens as we take small steps to share our pain with the Lord and ask for supernatural grace to forgive. He will be faithful to give us what our hearts need.

3. Forgive yourself. Many have gotten a sick heart and have stopped dreaming because of a series of personal failures. The hardest person to forgive is yourself. We usually hold ourselves to unrealistic standards and tend to punish ourselves when we don't live up to them. We are disregarding the fact that the cross of Jesus Christ is sufficient payment for our sins when we refuse to forgive ourselves. It is as if we are telling Jesus, "My self-inflicted punishment is a better ransom for my sins than what You did in sacrificing Your life for me on the cross." This is a perverted kind of self-salvation that exalts our works above the work of the cross. To live like this is to live under the heavy weight of shame and guilt.

4. Ask the Holy Spirit to reveal to you what lies you have believed. Hopelessness is built on a highly sophisticated network of lies that are sown into our hearts over a period of time. When we agree with the lies of the enemy, we empower him to bind us and to keep our hearts weak and anemic. The solution is to ask the Holy Spirit to expose the web of lies that we have agreed with and to break those agreements through repentance. This is not a mental exercise where we probe our brain to discover the lies. It is a supernatural work of the Holy Spirit where He turns on the light and exposes the works of darkness.

5. **Repent for believing the lies of the enemy**. As God shows what lies you have believed then simply break agreement with them by repenting for believing them.

6. **Replace the lies with truth**. Then ask the Holy Spirit to show you what truth He wants to replace the lie with. As He reveals truth to our inner man, the truth will set you free (John 8:32). The truth will be your sword as the enemy tempts you to believe his lies again.

The Practices of a Dreamer

Having revelation of who we are as dreamers is not enough. We must intentionally pursue the practices of a dreamer. I want to suggest a few practices that will position you to fulfill the wildest dreams of your heart with zeal and passion.

1. **Write down your dreams**. There is something powerful that happens when you get what's in your head onto paper. There's nothing that will motivate you more than putting language to your dreams for the first time. As you write down your dreams, suspend all limitations of time, money, and ability. A dream is not supposed to be a realistic, attainable five-year plan with specific action steps. A dream is composed of the raw guts of our deepest desires. Most people have never allowed themselves to move beyond their comfort zone because of fear. Suspend the voice of fear for just fifteen minutes and ask yourself, "What would I do if I had no fear and could do whatever I wanted?"

Don't stop after just one dream. I want to challenge you to write down one hundred dreams or desires. Don't be afraid to include fun things you've always wanted to do. Remember, your desires spring up out of your communion with God and are the product of your born-again nature. Many times we are immediately suspicious of the purity of our desires. Stop judging yourself and write them down. If you are on the wrong path the Holy Spirit will be faithful to show you.

2. **Read and meditate on your dreams on a regular basis.** Expand your dreams. Make them bigger. Water them with prayer and give the seeds of your desire room to grow and mature. Meditating on your dreams will keep the zeal stirred in your heart and also give the Holy Spirit an opportunity to help you work through any inner-struggles that come up as you dream.

3. **Share your dreams with someone who will fight for you**, encourage you and hold you accountable to fulfilling them. Ask the Lord to show you who to share with. Not everyone will honor your heart and champion your dreams. Having a friend to share the struggles and resistance you are facing will help you keep going when you feel like quitting.

4. **Read scripture and study books that are on the topic of what you are dreaming about**. This will keep the fires of your heart stoked and zealous to see your vision come to pass.

5. **Write down the prophetic words** spoken over your life and pray and declare them on a regular basis. The word of the Lord will energize you and keep you aligned with the truth.

6. **Get creative.** Find visual ways to remind yourself of your dreams.

You were created to be a hope-filled, zealous dreamer that impacts the earth with supernatural power. The world is groaning as it waits for you to step into the fullness of who you are as a son and daughter of God. Inside of you is the key to the world's problems. As you cultivate the dreams of your heart God will mature you, and ultimately position you to play your part in shifting the course of history and bringing His kingdom to earth.

Dreaming beckons us out of the slumber and numbness of the status quo and compels into the realm of the impossible where we co-labor with God to do extraordinary exploits. While the church slips away into a dreamless sleep, the tide of evil continues to sweep the nations. The statistics of abortion, pornography, divorce rates, suicide, and abuse demand that a new generation awakens from their spiritual coma and dreams, with eyes wide open, about what God longs to do in the earth. What could happen if a company of young people began to receive the dreams of heaven for their generation and act upon them? Let's find out!

About the Author

David Fritch currently serves on the senior leadership team of the Burn 24-7, and is the founder of the Burning Ones Missions Base in Oklahoma. The base hosts both full-time and part-time discipleship schools and sends out missionaries on short-term trips all over America and the nations. The cry of his heart is to see entire cities and nations transformed by the power of the gospel. The firm conviction that the restoration of night and day worship and prayer are a key ingredient to fulfillment of the great commission has fueled David to travel the world (including Asia, the Middle East, Europe, and Africa) to preach, teach, and equip the body of Christ to enter into this reality. Connect with David at www.davidfritch.com, www.burningones.com, or www.facebook.com/ypdave.

Chapter 4

Clear Out the Clutter

Caleb Klinge

As we journey through life, we can start to collect clutter. This is especially evident when it's time to move and that dreaded packing process begins. Suddenly we find ourselves asking, "Where did I get all of this stuff?" Garages, closets, and other storage areas accumulate belongings over time, and when a space is needed or it's time to move, decisions have to be made. In our household, we'll occasionally have a garage sale, donate, or give things away, or, when necessary, just throw them out. Most people will do something similar, but some are addicted to stockpiling belongings.

Reality television shows like *Hoarders* depict extreme examples of this. People are held hostage by the accumulation of junk in their own homes, sleeping on piles of items that they've hoarded because there is barely space to move. This often leads to serious health problems since the house is virtually impossible to clean. These individuals have actually developed a dependency on *stuff*. In their addiction, they are afraid to let their unnecessary possessions go and live in a free, open space. The things that people think they can't live without are preventing them from actually living. Interventions are necessary to rescue people right in their own houses.

Our lives can be the same way. The heart can become focused on materialism or distracted by lesser purposes instead of being fixed on God. Disappointments and unhealed hurts can accumulate over time. Unforgiveness and bitterness can slowly creep in. The things we think we can't let go are keeping us back from the abundant life Jesus came to give us. The space in our heart that is intended for God becomes occupied by clutter, diminishing fellowship with Him and hindering His purpose for our lives. An intervention is necessary for the heart to be restored.

I learned this by personal experience. I'm a pastor's kid who grew up in a Christian home. I've known the goodness of God and decided to follow Jesus at a very young age. I had everything going for me: parents who loved me, a great church and youth group, and friends that genuinely encouraged me. In spite of this, by the time I reached my freshman year of college, I was coasting spiritually. My story is not one of renouncing the Lord but of seeking other things rather than seeking the kingdom first. I didn't realize it, but my priorities were all wrong. Distance had developed in my relationship with Jesus, and I didn't recognize it even though people around me did.

There was a deep emptiness in my heart that began to grow stronger. The emptiness could only be filled with the presence of God, but as the emptiness grew, I tried to fill it with other things.

Initially, the more dissatisfied I became, the more I threw myself into surfing, music, and relationships. Since then, I've learned that when good things, including gifts from the Lord, become a substitute for Him, those things simply become clutter that displaces what really matters. I know now that I had been seeking refuge and comfort in my interests rather than in the Comforter. They were substitutes that couldn't satisfy. The more I filled my life with them, the emptier I became. I needed an intervention.

The intervention came in an unexpected way. My parents divorced, throwing my world into upheaval. I never thought this could happen to my Bible-believing, church-planting, Jesus-following parents that had given themselves to serve the Lord. This crisis stirred questions in my heart about what was real and what wasn't. I was tempted to allow the pain of the situation to become an excuse to go into the world and do my own thing, but I had experienced too much of God's presence to simply walk away from Him. Miraculously, in the midst of all the confusion and pain, a hunger for Jesus rose up in my heart. God began to draw me into the secret place. I decided to boldly seek the Lord for answers to the questions of my heart.

I let go of the things that I had been completely immersed in, including surfing and music. Instead, every day I set aside time to pray and to plunge myself in the Word. Gradually, seeking the Lord for answers shifted to seeking the Lord Himself. As these times of intimate fellowship grew, the emptiness in my heart began to get filled. At times it felt as if the tangible presence of God was filling my room. A passion for God began to burn in my heart. I had so much joy that I didn't even miss the things that I had let go of in that season. As I was shut away in the secret place, I discovered that Jesus is the only one that truly satisfies. He not only answered questions of my heart but also did something so much greater. God set my heart on fire for His kingdom and revealed that He had a purpose for my life far beyond anything I'd previously known. That season set me up for a life-changing encounter with God that I'll share about later in this chapter.

An Intervention in the House of the Lord

In hoarding situations, professional organizers come in to help decide what to throw away and what to keep. In kingdom life, there is an anointing to professionally organize and align our lives around what ultimately matters to the Father. This anointing is called the zeal of the Lord. With it comes the grace to *seek first* the King and His kingdom (Matthew 6:33) and to be launched into God's purpose.

Jesus intervened in His own house, the temple in Jerusalem, right after His first miracle at the wedding at Cana. He came into His house with zeal and went to work clearing out the clutter.

> Now the Passover of the Jews was at hand, and Jesus went up to Jerusalem. And He found in the temple those who sold oxen and sheep and doves, and the money changers doing business. When He had made a whip of cords, He drove them all out of the temple, with the sheep and the oxen, and poured out the changers' money and overturned the tables. And He said to those who sold doves, "Take these things away! Do not make My Father's house a house of merchandise!" Then His disciples remembered that it was written, "Zeal for Your house has eaten Me up."
>
> —John 2:13–17, NKJV

In this portion of scripture, we see a picture of heaven's priorities confronting earth's complacency. It's a picture of what God is doing in our personal lives and in His church today.

As Jesus cleared out the temple, His disciples *remembered* what was written in the Psalms about zeal. This is a key to how the Holy Spirit operates. He brings God's promises, purposes, and words to our remembrance. The words we remember become activated, and our hearts are stirred to walk in the Word (2 Peter 1:13).

> "But the Helper, the Holy Spirit, whom the Father will send in My name, He will teach you all things, and bring to your remembrance all things that I said to you." —John 14:26, NKJV

Today the Holy Spirit is bringing the Father's purpose to our remembrance. He is restoring zeal to our lives and calling us to be a people that live with holy passion.

Money Changers Displacing a Heart for the Nations

The temple of Israel was divided into several sections and various courts. Historical documentation shows that moneychangers and sellers of animals occupied the Court of the Gentiles. Israel had always been called to be a light to the nations. From the very beginning, God promised Abraham that through his descendants "all the families of the earth" would be blessed (Genesis 12:3, NKJV). The prophet Isaiah directly stated: "For My house shall be called a house of prayer for all nations" (Isaiah 56:7, NKJV).

When Jesus first entered the temple, He found them "doing business," but it wasn't the Father's business. He found that price-gouging moneychangers and merchants selling sacrificial animals had occupied the court that was dedicated as a place for nations to come and worship. The fact that they had displaced the area that gave Gentiles access to worship the God of Israel showed that they had completely forgotten what they were called to do.

Their activity was filling a space that God had designated for a different purpose. This is some very poignant symbolism. It pictures a church that has become cluttered and has allowed the Father's passion for reaching every tribe, tongue, and nation on the earth to be displaced by other activities. It pictures believers who have lost their hunger for God's presence and have become disconnected from God's purpose.

I'm sure no one woke up and said, "Let's fill the court of the Gentiles with an exchange bank and a farmers' market today." It's the same with our lives. It all begins with little compromises, small encroachments, and minor distractions. It's the "little foxes" that, unaddressed, "spoil the vine" (Song of Solomon 2:15, NKJV). Small encroachments give way to larger ones. Clutter tends to attract more clutter until the essential is displaced by the meaningless.

Clearing Clutter and Creating Space

Jesus' cleansing of the temple shows us what a gift zeal is. Zeal brings a divine intervention to remove all the debris that displaces God's purpose. The godly passion that comes from being in His Presence and knowing the Father's heart realigns our priorities and brings order to the house. Zeal creates space for what ultimately matters. It clears the clutter that slowly accumulates—clutter that we become accustomed and even blind to—making room for the agenda of the Father's heart.

Some associate the word *zeal* with legalism. The religious spirit seeks to hijack zeal and turn it into harsh legalism, but legalism has never advanced the kingdom. True zeal is the passion of the Father's heart imparted to our hearts. Passion brings the increase that legalism cannot.

> Of the increase of *His* government and peace *there will be* no end; upon the throne of David and over His kingdom, to order it and establish it with judgment and justice from that time forward, even forever. **The zeal of the Lord of hosts will perform this**.
>
> —Isaiah 9:7, NKJV

When zeal is imparted, a pure, holy flame roars to life. Zeal comes with grace to get our house in order, our priorities right, and our hearts realigned with God's purpose. It has a unique way of bringing clarity and helping us prioritize kingdom values.

In addition, zeal *propels us* forward in kingdom purpose. That's why it is so critical to never lack zeal in these last days. Zeal is extremely relevant to the end-time church. It is necessary for the church to bring in the last-days harvest, be the bride that has made herself ready, and prepare the way of the Lord.

For All Nations—My Encounter with the Holy Spirit

As I shared earlier, the Holy Spirit drew me into a season of seeking the Lord intensely for several months. As the clutter was cleared out, my heart came alive with joy and my emptiness was filled with His presence.

During that time, I went to a retreat for high school and college students. At the end of one of the morning meetings, God began moving and an altar call was given, inviting students into genuine repentance. I had already been in a season of repentance, but I responded anyway out of hunger. As I stood in line to receive prayer, I had an encounter with God that changed my life. Before anyone prayed for me, God showed me an open vision of nations and faces of people. Suddenly, He flooded my heart with love for them. I began to weep uncontrollably as I received the Father's love for these people groups. It was a love that rested on my heart like a weight.

The prayer line continued, and, after about fifteen minutes, I was finally at the front. I lifted my hands, and before anyone laid a hand on me, my arms began to shake involuntarily, and I experienced wave after wave of what felt like an electric current pulsing through my body. Twenty years ago, this encounter with God was a transformational moment that propelled me into ministry and missions. Shortly after this encounter, I decided to go to Bible college to prepare for a life of service for the King, and I haven't looked back since.

Because the precious space in my heart that had previously been filled with substitutes had been cleared, I was positioned to receive from the Father. In a moment, I received an impartation of love and passion from the Father's heart that simply wasn't there before. I wasn't even looking for it. I was just seeking Him.

A Finishing Anointing

The early church launched out, full of the Holy Spirit and fire, with a passion to take the Gospel of the kingdom to every nation. They started well. The baton has been handed down through the generations, and now it has been passed to us. Our generation is called to finish what was started. While the zeal of the Lord removes clutter and unnecessary weight from our hearts, Hebrews 12:1 reveals that it also empowers us to run the race God has set before us and complete our God given assignments.

> Therefore we also, since we are surrounded by so great
> a cloud of witnesses, let us lay aside every weight, and

the sin which so easily ensnares us, and let us run
with endurance the race that is set before us.

—Hebrews 12:1, NKJV

The zeal of the Lord doesn't just help us *prepare* to run. His zeal
empowers us to run the race and finish strong. At the beginning
of a marathon, an endurance athlete is filled with excitement and
adrenaline, and often begins with a fast pace. This can be equated
to the initial faith that we have when we first receive vision from
the Lord, hear His promises, and discover His purpose. When a
marathoner comes to the final portion of the course, there's another surge of adrenaline, sometimes referred to as a "kick." New
strength kicks in to finish the course, a strength that is different
than the excitement at the beginning. Here, the athlete decides to
give everything they have and press for the finish line.

We are entering the final leg of the race. The Lord is revealing Himself to us not only as the Alpha, the First, and the Beginning. He's revealing Himself as the Omega, the Last, and the
End. He is not just the Author. He is the Finisher. The zeal of the
Lord is coming upon the church so she can finish strong. She will
not have a weak finish, limping across the finish line. Rather, the
church will lay aside every weight that holds her back, recover lost
ground, and finish victorious. As the Lord anoints her with zeal,
she will say, like the great Scottish Olympian Eric Liddel, "When
I run, I feel His pleasure."

A Smoldering Wick He Will Not Quench

The Lord has a fresh impartation of zeal for you as you behold
the One whose eyes are as a flame of fire. The more we spend time
beholding Him in worship and prayer, the more our hearts are

fanned into a flame. This zeal has its source in intimacy with God alone. It can't be manufactured; it is something we must steward. Daily, we must choose to live with His heart as our first priority, staying in fellowship with the Master. That is why Scripture says, "Keep your heart with all diligence, for out of it *spring* the issues of life" (Proverbs 4:23, NKJV).

Perhaps discouragement, disillusionment, or deferred hope have made you vulnerable to distraction or to interests that do not serve the holy calling God has called you with. Perhaps your heart has become full of clutter, and you need an intervention.

Remember that God is for you! There is always hope. Know this: "A smoldering wick he will not quench (Matthew 12:20, ESV)." The Lord stands ready to fan the smoldering embers in your heart back into full flame. He is the Source. Jesus said that the Holy Spirit "will take of what is Mine, and declare it unto you." The Holy Spirit is once again declaring, revealing, and imparting the zeal of the Lord of Hosts to this generation. Right now, you can allow the Holy Spirit to fill the deep places of your heart with His zeal again.

Make this simple prayer your own today:

> Lord Jesus, I open my heart to You now and invite You to intervene in my life. Clear out the clutter that displaces my fellowship with You and the priorities of Your heart. Breathe on me again by Your Spirit, and cause my heart to be fanned into flame. Just as You spoke to the Laodicean church to "be zealous and repent," I receive grace from You now to do the same. In the name of Jesus. Amen.

About the Author

Caleb Klinge is the lead pastor at New Life Christian Center in Novato, California, together with his wife Rachel. Located in Marin County, just north of the Golden Gate in the San Francisco Bay Area, they are passionate for an invasion of God's presence and kingdom that brings regional and global transformation. In addition to ministry in California, Caleb has served in ministry extended periods in Brazzaville, Congo, and Siberia, Russia. His ministry is used by the Lord to release faith, encouragement, and breakthrough. Caleb and Rachel have been married for seventeen years and have two children, Benjamin and Phebe. Caleb also serves as an apostolic leader and board member of the grassroots worship, prayer, and mission movement, Burn 24-7. Contact him at www.visitnewlife.com or calebk@theburn247.com.

Chapter 5

Vision for Pursuit

Corey Russell

From day one of my salvation, revival has been in my blood. My first six months in the kingdom occurred during a supernatural move of the Holy Spirit where I experienced the manifest presence of God on a regular basis and saw many souls saved and lives transformed.

This experience dramatically marked my life. After seeing His power, feeling His presence, and receiving His love, I was determined to be a man who knew God. I didn't want to just know about Him or know people who knew Him. I had to know God for myself. I was captured by the vision of pursuing the knowledge of God. Now, sixteen years later, I am convinced that the key to maintaining fervency and a fiery spirit for decades is found in vision.

The Power of Vision

The truth is that everything in life is fueled by vision. We determine what we want in the arenas of work, fitness, finances, and relationships, and then we take the necessary steps to achieve our goals. This is how we live. In Proverbs 29:18, Solomon declares that without vision the people perish. When it comes to sustaining the fire of love for God, one of the greatest and most overlooked dangers is the lack of vision. If we lack clarity concerning what we want and where we are going in God, we are quickly knocked off course and end up settling for something far less than what God intended.

This is a simple principle, yet so often in the Christian life we fail to live by it. One of the primary reasons that we see so many falling stars in the church—people who burned brightly for God in their twenties but then gradually pulled back and settled into complacency as the pressures of life increased—is due to a lack of vision. In our early years of salvation, everything is brand new: God is transforming our lives and revealing His heart. But as we transition from our twenties to our thirties, get married, have kids, and take on the demands of mortgages and bills, often our hearts get smaller. God is no longer the focus of our life; we are spread thin and distracted. Eventually, the pressures of our careers, relationships, and finances overwhelm our commitments to prayer, fasting, and reading the Word.

I have felt this temptation in my own life, and I have seen it played out in the lives of many. The fire that burned in their youth becomes a distant memory, and as another decade goes by, they actually begin to disdain and speak against the radical commitment of those early years. Jesus Himself warned that the cares of this life will extinguish the flame if we do not have a specific vision to guide us (Mark 4:18–19).

Having Vision to Pursue the Knowledge of God

When I think of living a life consumed by the vision to know God, I think of the apostle Paul. He was converted after he received a vision on the road to Damascus. He saw the resurrected Lord with his own eyes, and that encounter left him blind for three days. Though he recovered his physical sight, he never recovered from the experience. Paul traveled all over the known world proclaiming the gospel, but his entire life was spent on that road to Damascus, pursuing the glorious Man who called him by name.

I have heard it said if we could see what Paul saw, we would be empowered to live as he lived. In Philippians 3, Paul opened his heart and revealed the vision that possessed his life. It sustained him through poverty and abundance, adversity and prosperity, ill health, persecution, and a multitude of other trials (2 Corinthians 11:23–29). After stating his credentials as a Pharisee, he says:

> Yet indeed I also count all things loss for **the excellence of the knowledge of Christ Jesus my Lord…that I may know Him** and the power of His resurrection, and the fellowship of His sufferings, being conformed to His death, if, by any means, I may attain to the resurrection from the dead.
>
> —Philippians 3:8, 10–11, NKJV

Paul was gripped by the vision of knowing Christ. The encounter on the road to Damascus destroyed all of his pride, his vain pursuits and striving for recognition, and his temporal goals and pleasures. Everything was consumed by "the excellence of the knowledge of Christ Jesus." This is the only vision big enough to sustain us through every season of life. When we allow lesser goals to take first place in our hearts, we end up disillusioned and burned out.

Too often we think we are running after the knowledge of God, but when we are passed over for promotion or our ministry doesn't take off as planned, we discover what we are really living for and pursuing. At the end of the day, God will not cater to our agendas. Instead, He allows disappointments to reveal the secret ambitions and offenses in our hearts. Our vision cannot be success in ministry, or the wife and kids, or freedom from financial worries. Everything must take second place to knowing God.

In Psalm 27:4, David wrote, "One thing I have desired of the Lord, that will I seek: that I may dwell in the house of the Lord all the days of my life, to behold the beauty of the Lord, and to inquire in His temple" (NKJV). Like Paul, David was a man consumed by the vision of knowing God. The only thing he wanted in life was to dwell in God's presence and see His face.

This same desire is expressed in John 17, when Jesus prayed for His disciples. In this incredible passage, we are allowed to eavesdrop on God the Son as He shares the deepest longings of His heart with God the Father. In verse 24, He declares, "Father, I desire that they also whom You gave Me may be with Me where I am, that they may behold My glory which You have given Me" (NKJV). This is the same vision articulated by David. His "one thing" desire is actually answering Jesus' prayer for eternal communion. We were created to be satisfied with nothing less than the knowledge of God, and our pursuit of this vision in turn satisfies the deepest desires of God's heart.

After sharing this same vision in Philippians 3:8-11, Paul proceeds to describe how he pursues the knowledge of God. I believe these verses reveal the secret to sustaining a fresh fire in the heart for decades.

> Not that I have already attained, or am already perfected; but I press on, that I may lay hold of that for which Christ Jesus has also laid hold of me. Brethren, I do not count myself to have apprehended; but one thing I do, forgetting those things which are behind and reaching forward to those things which are ahead, I press toward the goal for the prize of the upward call of God in Christ Jesus. —Philippians 3:12–14, NKJV

Look at the verb phrases in this passage: press on, lay hold of, forget, reach forward, and press toward. These are the actions that characterized Paul's pursuit of God. He understood that God had already laid hold of him in salvation, and in return he laid hold of God, determined to reach, press, and wrestle to attain the fullness of His calling in this age and the next.

Notice that, as a mature apostle, Paul said he had not attained his goal. At the end of his life, his statement was that he had not arrived. His vision was eternal—it was far greater than anything in this life—and therefore he gave his life to pursue the eternal. Paul then highlighted the practical actions that sustained his pursuit. The first is forgetting his failures and successes.

In this journey of reaching forward, the past can be the greatest obstacle to our future. Most of us are held back by our failures, whether they are moral failures, relational failures, or breakdowns. There are many believers who feel stuck in a spiritual time-out because of something they did five years ago. Despite their repentance, they never *feel* worthy enough for God and are locked up in fear. But Paul declared he would not live in the tragedies and triumphs of yesterday. He lived his life forgetting those things that were behind, receiving the forgiveness of Jesus at face value, and moving forward.

He also forgot his successes. Paul had an impressive resume: he authored most of the New Testament; his preaching led to the salvation of twenty-five thousand souls in Ephesus alone; he moved in mighty signs and wonders; and he received many divine revelations and visitations. Yet he did not dwell on his career highlights. This is a key point; we cannot live in the memory of where we were five years ago convinced it is a present-tense reality. Instead, we must reach forward to those things that are ahead and press on to know God. This reaching forward characterized the mature apostle's walk. I like to ask myself, "Is there a fresh reach in my spirit, or am I subscribing to theology that perpetually lets me rest?"

> Therefore let us, as many as are mature, have this mind; and if in anything you think otherwise, God will reveal even this to you. Nevertheless, to the degree that we have already attained, let us walk by the same rule, let us be of the same mind.
>
> —Philippians 3:15–16, NKJV

Paul concludes this glorious passage by stating that mature Christians understand going after God requires reaching, forgetting, and pressing. "Therefore let us, as many as are mature, have this mind"—in other words—"think this way." This is the way a mature believer thinks: set your mind on God, forget your successes and failures, and press on. He then addresses those who disagree with this statement, and declares that God will chase them down and convince them of these truths. False grace is actually a sign of immaturity, but Paul won't fight about this point—he leaves room for the Holy Spirit to release revelation.

"Nevertheless, to the degree we have already attained, let us walk by the same rule, let us be of the same mind." Here Paul states that we must persevere and continue to do those things that escorted us into the knowledge of God in past seasons. This has been one of the greatest keys to fervency in my own life. The things I did in my early days, I do today. Jesus calls this the "first works" in His exhortation to the church of Ephesus (Revelation 2:4–5). Doing the first works of pursuing the knowledge of God ignites our first love and sustains our vision.

Having Vision of God's Pursuit of Us

The vision to know God consumed me from day one of my salvation, but my preconceived ideas about the journey were blown up a year later. I thought I would go from glory to glory, experiencing constant bliss and unending revelation. Instead, I ran headlong into the weakness of my flesh and the pain of disillusionment. What I did not realize at the time was that this actually prepared me to receive the greatest revelation of my life.

A year into my walk with God, I met the woman who is now my wife. We felt strongly led by God at the outset of the relationship and knew very quickly that we were going to get married. However, as things progressed we entered into a six-month period where those around us questioned our relationship and released confusing "prophetic words." This created a great deal of turmoil, doubt, and pain in our lives. I felt unable to do anything right, and this feeling opened the door to many mistakes and failures. I did not understand how the glory of my first year with God could vanish so quickly. I felt disqualified and useless. I was in school at the time, and I remember going to the bathroom between classes and crying. My belief in my own strength and zeal had utterly collapsed.

When I finally came out of that season, I vowed that I would never let God down again. I remember telling the Lord, "I don't know who that was, but here I am—a new man! From this day forward I will be Your guy." For the first two years of my marriage, I was incredibly driven. The fear of letting God down again haunted me. Fasting, praying, preaching—I threw myself into the pursuit of God. Although there was grace resting on my life in that season, I thought if I ever let up, I would backslide. I was afraid of becoming a statistic: another young guy who was on fire and then flamed out. I ran hard after God by His grace, but I was tormented internally. During that period of time, my wife and I moved to Kansas City and joined the International House of Prayer where the anointing on my life for fasting and prayer intensified. I did not realize fear was also in the mix. But God was after my heart.

In the summer of 2001, I was given an opportunity to minister in Norway. My wife felt strongly that I was supposed to go on this trip, so we emptied our bank account and bought the plane ticket. I was there for seven days, but only preached in the mornings. This meant I was alone in my room, twelve hours a day, for seven days. I was alone with God, and He began to bring me back to that season of failure and pain I experienced during my engagement. He told me that I was missing the most important revelation I would ever receive. I was trying to forget the pain of the past, but God wanted to meet me in that place and reveal His heart. He supernaturally drew me into John 13–14, and placed me in Peter's shoes. The revelation that transformed Peter's life became the revelation that transformed mine.

In John 13–17, we witness the events of the final hours before Jesus' arrest, trial, and execution. Jesus washes His disciples' feet, releases Judas to betray Him, and then begins to prepare the remaining disciples for His departure. These young men had given up everything to follow Jesus: for over three years they walked with Him, talked with Him, and were utterly dependent on His presence. So when Jesus announced that He was going away and they could not come with Him, they were shocked and grieved. They still expected their Messiah to reveal Himself as a conquering king; the idea that He would suffer and die was confusing and offensive.

Peter said to Him, "Lord, why can I not follow You now? I will lay down my life for Your sake" (John 13:37, NKJV). Peter responded with the cry of a sincere disciple. Like David, his greatest desire was to be with Jesus. However, his methodology was wrong. He thought the only way to keep up with Jesus was to display unique love, dedication, and sacrifice. Peter wanted to distinguish himself from everyone else and earn his place at Jesus' side. Though he had followed Jesus for three years, he still trusted in his own zeal and commitment. In John 13, Jesus responded to Peter tenderly, but with great honesty:

> Jesus answered him, "Will you lay down your life for My sake? Most assuredly, I say to you, the rooster shall not crow till you have denied Me three times."
>
> —John 13:38, NKJV

In other words, "I really love your heart, but you are not as dedicated to Me as you think you are. I am going to lay down My life for your sake, but you are going to fail Me more miserably than anyone who has ever lived on the most important night of human history. You will deny Me three times."

Immediately after this, Jesus encouraged His zealous young disciple with these words:

> Let not your heart be troubled; you believe in God,
> believe also in Me. In my Father's house are many
> mansions; if it were not so, I would have told you. I
> go to prepare a place for you. And if I go and prepare
> a place for you, I will come again and receive you to
> Myself; that where I am, there you may be also.
> —John 14:1–3, NKJV

There must come a point in our pursuit of God where we cease to live out of our own strength and begin to live out of the overflow of His pursuit of us. I believe we all must experience this breakdown, just as Peter did. It is only after our greatest attempts to keep up with God have failed miserably that we are ready to receive the revelation of the cross.

When we behold Jesus hanging on a tree, dying for us, our religious pride, self-sufficiency, and independence are exposed, and we are confronted with the truth that we cannot do a single thing to add to our standing before God. The core fear that drove Peter was that there would not be room for him in the Father's house unless he made a place for himself.

Peter believed he had to display unique devotion and dedication. But there are no superheroes in the body of Christ. We are all weak, broken, and in need of a Savior. The cross is the great equalizer. When we fall short, there is a Man hanging on a tree, dying. When we are unable to give anything, He gives everything.

Jesus' message to Peter was one of hope: "You believe in God, believe also in Me. Take your eyes off yourself and look at Me because I am going to carry you through this." To emphasize this reality, Jesus stated that He would tell us if it were otherwise. "If it were not so, I would have told you. If you were required to show unique devotion and unparalleled zeal, I would let you know. Understand that everyone falls short of My standards, but I am going to prepare a place in My Father's house and do for you what you cannot do yourself." Christianity is not a competitive sport. The people who humble themselves and let Jesus carry them receive the kingdom.

In spite of Jesus' warning, Peter fell hard. Although he had received direct revelation from the Father concerning Jesus' identity and had witnessed the glory of the Son on the Mount of Transfiguration, he buckled under pressure when questioned by a young girl on the night of Jesus' arrest. In Luke's gospel, it says that after his third denial, the Lord turned and looked at him (Luke 22:61).

Can you imagine what it felt like to hear the rooster crow and then see the broken, bloody face of Jesus? Can you imagine what the three days between the crucifixion and the resurrection were like for Peter? His faith in Jesus and in himself was completely shattered. I doubt he could conceive of a way to salvage his life as a disciple, and so he returned to his former trade as a broken and weak man. Yet Jesus' prayer carried him through that dark season:

> "Simon, Simon! Indeed, Satan has asked for you, that
> he may sift you as wheat. But I have prayed for you,
> that your faith should not fail; and when you have
> returned to Me, strengthen your brethren."
>
> —Luke 22:31–32, NKJV

Peter could not see it at the time, but the power of that prayer prepared his heart for restoration.

After the resurrection, Jesus purposefully pursued Peter in order to speak to those places of disillusionment, pain, and weakness within him. In John 21, we see that for each denial Jesus affirmed his love, breaking the power of the enemy's lies and torment, and commissioning Peter to feed His sheep. Fifty days later, the same man who could not confront a young girl by a campfire stood up and preached the first message of the Church. Three thousand were saved. This is the key to sustaining zeal: Peter received the revelation that he had a place in the Father's house regardless of his weakness.

And this same revelation transformed my life. During my week in Norway, I became Peter. Through the story of his commitment, failure, and restoration, Jesus addressed the deepest places of fear, shame, and guilt in my heart. He met me in those places, washed me, and brought me into the Father's house. For two years, I had been trying to establish my own righteousness, but the Lord wanted to encounter me in my nothingness. I finally came face to face with the One who wanted me, even when I failed and came up short. I have no doubt that this revelation saved my life, my marriage, my family, and my ministry. Though I had been walking with the Lord, I was living outside of the Father's house. During those seven days I was transferred into the Father's house—into a new place of intimacy, rest, and authority.

This encounter changed the way I pursued God, broke the power of fear in my life, delivered me from an orphan spirit, and ushered me into the experiential reality of sonship—a reality I am continuing to grow in to this day. There are always deeper places in the human heart that need to encounter the power of the cross and the love of the Father. However, this initial breakthrough set me on a course that has sustained me for the past fourteen years of ministry.

Running in His Hand

In Psalm 63:8, David says, "My soul follows close behind You; Your right hand upholds me" (NKJV). David was a man of vision who pursued God with all of his strength, but he also understood the grace and mercy of the Father. This verse articulates both the need for tenacity and vision and the confidence that comes from resting in God's pursuit of our lives. These two principles, when walked out consistently, will sustain real fire for decades. Many believers want to choose one over the other, but both are necessary.

The vision to pursue the knowledge of God by running hard after Him is expressed in the first half of the verse: "My soul follows close behind You." This is the spiritual violence Jesus spoke of in Matthew 11:12 when He told the disciples that the kingdom was available to those who took hold of it forcefully. Hungry, spiritually violent people receive things from Jesus that others do not. Complacency is one of the greatest enemies we must overcome in order to remain close to God. We must cultivate hunger, tenacity, and vision if we want to maintain a burning heart.

However, the second portion of Psalm 63:8 speaks of being unconditionally loved and accepted by the Father: "Your right hand upholds me." In other words, God holds us as we run after Him. We are running in the palm of His hand.

I like to think of this as pursuing God from a place of rest. It is a necessary tension in the life of a believer. We need a revelation of the God who is upholding and sustaining us, or our hearts will shut down and we will fall into striving and religion. But we also need a revelation of the God who requires us to rise up and lay hold of Him.

This is the twofold anchor for our souls. God is going to bring us through, but we cannot use that as license to get into our La-Z-Boy chair. He brings us forth because we come forth. It is a paradox. We cannot have one reality without the other; the tension between the two truths protects us from burnout and complacency.

In John 10, Jesus says that no one is able to snatch anyone out of the Father's hand. Jesus' prayer in John 17 illustrates this reality too. There is a prayer over my life and yours: "Keep them in Your name. I have kept them, and I am going to keep them in Your name." Jesus is praying before the Father right now, saying "I want them to be with Me where I am."

This strength is greater than yours or mine. Our strength is a byproduct of touching His strength. We have to live in this place. John 17 is the prayer that upholds us; there is a hand upholding, covering, and bringing us forth in love.

Jude 24 says, "Now to Him who is able to keep you from stumbling, and to present you faultless before the presence of His glory with exceeding joy" (NKJV). This is our security; it frees us to run after God. We were not made to simply pursue God. We were made to live out of the overflow of His pursuit of us.

About the Author

Corey Russell currently serves on the senior leadership team of the International House of Prayer (IHOP–KC) as he has since 2001. Corey is the Director of the Forerunner Program at the International House of Prayer University (IHOPU), discipling and training young preachers and leaders. He travels nationally and internationally preaching on themes of knowledge of God, intercession, and the forerunner ministry. He resides in Kansas City with his wife, Dana, and their three daughters. He has written several books (*Pursuit of the Holy*, *Glory Within*, and *Ancient Paths*) as well as released three preaching CDs ("Days of Noah," "Ancient Paths," and "Eyes Opened"). You can get more information about Corey and his ministry at www.coreyrussell.org.

Chapter 6

A Burning Flame

Faytene Grasseschi

Zeal. I believe this is one of the most powerful words in the English language.

Zeal has conquered kingdoms, established nations, and re-formed societies. It has turned the world upside-down time and time again—and it will do it again. Capture zeal and you have captured so much more. In capturing zeal you have gained the ability to profoundly impact the world. Furthermore, if your zeal is powered by the greatest Source that exists—God—you have now become atomically powerful.

Zeal. Get it. Keep it. Use it for the King's fame.

I see it like this: One life is all you have; you live it and it is gone. But to live with our God's fire and purpose in your soul is more terrible than dying, even more terrible than dying young

69

(paraphrased from Joan of Arc). I love feeling the zeal of heaven pulsating though my body like fire shut up in my bones.

When I consider zeal, there are two primary lines of questioning that come to mind. Firstly, what is the source? Where does godly zeal truly come from? How do you get it if you don't have it? What triggers it?

The second line of questioning is this: Once you have found it, how do you keep it? What fuels it for the long haul? Furthermore, how do you not only keep it, but also grow in it from season to season?

I don't want to be lit on fire like a booming flare only to fizzle out moments later. I want to burn for life. I want to burn forever. *A burner for life*—that is what I want to be. If you are reading this, then I trust this is the hunger of your soul as well.

So that is where I want to go with you in these few pages we have together. How do you get zeal? But more than that—how do you keep it?

He Is the King of Zeal

When talking about the source of zeal, we must remember that zeal is an attribute of God Himself. Isaiah 42:13 says that God stirs up His zeal like a warrior who then defeats His enemies. In Isaiah 37:32, the Word explains that **the zeal of the Lord** will accomplish the bringing forth of His remnant in the earth. The Hebrew word for zeal in these contexts is *hanq*, which means *ardor, jealousy* (as in a man's jealousy for his bride), *and anger against one's opponent*. God is jealous for His people. He is angry at the enemy and his works. He is a person of intense passion. Zeal is a part of who He is. It is a part of His nature.

What does this mean for us? Well, one of the things it means is that if zeal is a part of His nature then, as His sons and daughters, we can ask Him to impart, or increase, that attribute in us. Every good thing comes from our Father in heaven. If you want zeal, or if you want to grow in zeal, all you need to do is ask, receive by faith and then start to walk in it by faith. Our Father in heaven knows how to give good gifts to His children. I believe He will give us zeal if we only ask.

So, why don't we do just that?

> God, we love You, we love everything about You. We love Your zeal as it is a part of Your very nature. We know that You are a good Father who gives good gifts to His children. Because of this, we come to You boldly right now and, in joyful faith, ask You to impart a fresh and increased portion of Your zeal into our lives. Give us Your perspective in a way that will zealously propel us forward for Your glory. Give us Your heart that is zealous for the lost and the establishment of Your kingdom. Father, give us the very zeal of the Lord of hosts. Bring it on. In Jesus' name, amen.

That's a great start. Take a greater measure by faith.

Be Zealous, All the Time

The New Testament sheds a different angle on zeal than the Old Testament. Where the Old Testament points to God as the warrior of zeal, the New Testament calls on the believer to emulate this part of God's nature in their daily lives.

Romans 12:11 exhorts us to never be lacking in zeal but keep our spiritual fervor serving the Lord.

The Greek word for zeal here is *spoude*, which means *to be earnest, diligent, in a hurry, focused on accomplishing something, promoting or striving towards something*. This New Testament word for zeal is all about action, a sense of urgency, focus, and diligence. What an awesome challenge. We are called to live this kind of life constantly. That is awesome, but it requires God's empowerment.

Once our zeal is unlocked, God's empowerment can only truly flow through our lives if our focus and motivation is on track with His. Our focus harmonizes with His when we have intimate fellowship with Him. Only then will we experience the release of an unquenchable fire and an unhindered flow of His grace. When we are one with Him in heart and focus, His zeal naturally flows through us in an unhindered way. It all comes back to intimate unity with His heart. When we burn for what He burns for— when we burn for His kingdom purpose—His zeal becomes like an unquenchable river of fire in our bones.

Zealous for the Right Kingdom

I met the first love of my life, Jesus Christ, in 1995. I was twenty years old, in university, and had my whole life in front of me. Prior to this encounter, I was zealous for many things.

I suppose you could say I was a naturally driven and ambitious person, whether in school, sports, work, or in my personal life. At that time, I was definitely a burner—I was just burning for things that would simply burn up in eternity. Looking back, I can see clearly that there was a deep inner void in my soul that I was unconsciously trying to fill. The reality is that we are made for love, affirmation, and acceptance. Because of that, if we have not encountered the acceptance of our heavenly Father God, we will naturally strive for the approval of the world around us. It is human nature. Without God we are naturally driven to find something in life that will give us a sense of comfort and security—that was my story. Moreover, I think it just may be the story of most in our generation.

Fleshly zeal has been the story of mankind ever since Adam was driven from the Father's presence in the Garden of Eden. Additionally, it has increasingly become the story of this generation. Sociologically and spiritually we have been a fatherless generation running zealously after anything that would grant us a shred of security or affirmation. Some people call this an orphan spirit.

This drive to fill an affirmation void will express itself differently in different people's lives. For me, it expressed itself in the relentless pursuit of affirmation through sports accomplishments, academic achievements, and my social life. A casual on-looker might have looked at me and thought, "Hey, there is a young lady who is really going somewhere and has her stuff together." The reality, however, is that the motivation of my zeal was a root of insecurity. Because of this, my zeal was all about myself. It was totally self-focused. Sometimes this type of zeal is called *selfish ambition* or *performance orientation*.

As those that have been groomed in a fatherless culture, we have to ask ourselves: what is the source of our zeal? Why do we do what we do? Why do we charge forth for the kingdom? Why do we want the power of God flowing through our lives? Why do we crank it up when a microphone is in our hand? Is it because there is still a little orphan in our hearts that is looking for someone to notice and clap? Or is our zeal truly motivated by a humble desire to bring the Lamb the full reward of His sacrifice? These are important questions to ask when pressing in for more.

When pondering these questions in the light of my pre-Jesus zeal, I can say for sure before I met Him my zeal was all about me.

Before I met Jesus in 1995, I thought I was a Christian. I believed in God and prayed when I needed something. However, I never considered His heart or desires, nor did I have a daily connection with Him through His Spirit. When I met Him through the witness and prayers of several close friends, I was forever changed. It was like someone turned the lights on in my soul and I could see that Jesus was who He said He was. He was God. He was awesome. He was loving, kind, beautiful, and amazing—everything I had ever longed for. That is who He was.

I had found Someone worth living for. Not only that, but I had found security in the arms of God who knew me perfectly and loved me unconditionally. The revelation that I was His girl—and nothing could change that—flooded my soul. A waterfall of security and peace rushed over my being as I realized that He was mine, I was His, and that this was never going to change. I was completely, totally, massively loved and accepted by the One I could hide nothing from. Something shifted in my inner man. I was filled with His Spirit and a love, joy, peace—an ecstasy—filled my soul. I knew I would never be the same.

All I wanted to care about was what He cared about. All I wanted to burn for was what He burned for. In an instant, at the touch of His love, my inner motivation was completely re-aligned from an earthly focus to a heavenly one. I can remember in those early days praying this prayer, "God, when I close my eyes I want to see eternity stamped on my eyelids." I meant it. There was a God-given fire in my soul to live for the other side.

In many ways, I was the same Faytene. I had drive, energy, and ambition. The difference was that my entire worldview and motivation in life had radically shifted. When I looked at people, I no longer looked at them through the lens of, "Do they like me?

What do they think of me? What did they think about what I just said or did?" When I looked at people, I saw hell—literally sometimes. What I mean by this is that when I looked at people, I saw that they needed Jesus. If they did not find Him, they would be sentenced to a life of eternal darkness. This revelation was a game changer for me. I was deeply driven, by love, to tell as many people as I could about this awesome man Jesus that had saved me from myself, and saved me from hell.

A Source of Zeal: Revelation of Eternity

I believe that one of the most effective igniters and sustainers of true godly zeal is a revelation of eternity. I don't mean heaven. I mean eternity.

In our stream in the Body of Christ you hear a lot of talk about heaven. I love heavenly encounters. I love having them. I love hearing about them. I love worship. I love soaking. I love the glory. I love the atmosphere of heaven. I love sensing the reality of heaven's activity and having deeper insight into His throne room.

At the same time, though, while I have seen heavenly encounters transform people, I have not always seen it produce godly zeal that motivates people to outwardly focused action for the kingdom. I want to be careful and emphasize that I am not saying that I have *never* seen it produce godly zeal—I have just not *always* seen it produce godly zeal. I believe that this is because a revelation of the reality of heaven, void of some level of revelation of the reality of hell, is an incomplete revelation of eternity. An incomplete revelation will naturally affect behavior. We act out of what we know. We need to know that both heaven and hell are real. It sounds so basic, but to be honest, I find this worldview to be pretty rare.

Heaven is real and it is awesome. You want to go there.

Hell is real and it is horrific. Neither you nor anyone you know wants to go there.

Sometimes I pray easy prayers like this, "God please show me heaven." At other times I pray crazy prayers like this, "God please show me hell."

Why the second and not just the first? For me, the second fuels zeal.

It reminds me that time is ticking. It reminds me that Jesus came, lived, was ridiculed, tortured, and crucified for souls. It reminds me that I am His messenger and He is shouting from heaven, "Go get them! Go get them! Go get them! I love them. I died for them. I still weep for them. Go get them! Time is short."

If you love Him, you listen.

Hell Is Real

I will never forget the day when God crashed in on my world in such a real way with this revelation. It changed me.

I was taking a lunch break from my ministry position with a citywide mercy ministry to the poor. I had dashed out to one of my favorite stops just a few blocks from the church to nab a slice of pizza before heading back to the office to keep working for Jesus and the poor of the city. This day there was a nice man behind the counter who was of Middle Eastern descent. I smiled, greeted him, and indicated the piece of pizza I wanted. I watched him as he lifted it off the large pizza pan and onto a paper plate and my spirit immediately flashed to a vision.

In the vision, I saw this very man burning in hell in eternity. There was darkness, fire, and the intensity of evil all around. In the vision, his eyes locked onto my eyes and he looked at me with a pleading voice saying, "Why didn't you tell me?" Then, in a flash, it was over. I was struck to the core.

I was not sure what to say at that moment or how to bridge the conversation from, "Here is my money, thanks for the pizza," to, "Excuse me sir, but I just saw you burning in hell." I stood there with a blank stare, trying to get myself together. The man could tell I was visibly shaken by something. I silently gave him my money. He gave me the change and stood looking at me.

Gripped by what I had just seen, and a deep sense of responsibility for his soul, I took a risk and asked, "Sir, can I tell you what I just saw?" He replied, "Yes, please tell me." I said, "Sir, I just saw a vision of you burning in hell...do you believe in God?" He told me that he did and we went on to have a dialogue where I was able to share the Gospel with him. Right there, over the pizza counter, he told me that He wanted to give His life to Jesus. It was incredible. I was so thankful for God's mercy stopping me in my tracks for this man.

God is constantly on a rescue mission. He is zealous for the souls of mankind. It is the whole reason He came to earth. Since the Garden of Eden, there has been a contest for the souls of mankind. That contest still rages today. I don't know about you, but that revelation fires me up. It is an automatic zeal injection that propels me to run even harder in honor of our King Jesus' sacrifice.

Heaven Is Real

Before I close out this section on the revelation of eternity as a source of zeal, it is worth talking a bit more about heaven.

The beauty of this kingdom life is that it is free. He gave it all so we could have it all and live the dream with Him. Salvation is by grace, less no man should boast. This is true, indisputable, and clear in the Word. We can't get there of our own works—not even the best of us.

We do not get to heaven via our zealous works for God; however, that does not mean that we are to throw the proverbial "good works" baby out with the bathwater. Though our good works can't get us to heaven, the Word is also clear that our good works will follow us to heaven. This kingdom reality also deeply motivates me. I don't want a big house on earth. I want a big house in heaven. Some might say that this kind of thinking is a re-birth of performance orientation with a Jesus sticker on it. I don't believe it is. I believe that to live for treasure in heaven is simply wisdom. I want to run as the apostle Paul exhorted us to: in a way so as to win the prize. Let me give you few scriptures to back up what I am getting at.

Matthew 6:19 says that we are not to store up treasure in heaven where moth and rust destroy but we are to be givers that lay up treasure in heaven. Our zeal to give for God (financially) in the earth will follow us into heaven. Wow. Amazing. It is important to give generously on earth, as it will follow you to heaven. That motivates me. I want to throw as much as I can to the other side where it will never be destroyed.

1 Corinthians 3:12–15 (NIV) says that every single thing we do in the realm of time will be tested in the fire of God's perspective.

> If anyone builds on this foundation using gold, silver, costly stones, wood, hay or straw, their work will be shown for what it is, because the Day will bring it to light. It will be revealed with fire, and the fire will test the quality of each person's work. If what has been built survives, the builder will receive a reward. If it is burned up, the builder will suffer loss but yet will be saved—even though only as one escaping through the flames.

Those things we did with a pure motivation of godly zeal will stand for eternity. Those things we did for ourselves, our selfish ambition, will burn up in an instant. To me, that is deeply motivating. I don't think any of us want to waste our lives. I, as I am sure you do too, want to spend my life in such a way so that when my works are tested, they will stand up in the light of God's perspective and by His grace. This ignites a deep zeal in my soul. It reminds me that it matters how I live my life today.

Revelation 19:8 says that the Bride has made herself ready and is dressed in white linens for her heavenly wedding banquet. That gown is her righteous acts. Not only do her righteous acts follow her to eternity but she (we) wear them in eternity. The life you live you will wear forever. Wow. That is both intense and incredible. It is, I believe, one of the most powerful imparters of godly zeal.

There is nothing wrong with wanting to be great in heaven. The good news is that there is actually a built-in protection mechanism because if we don't do what we do for Him it will all burn anyway. You can't be selfishly motivated and great in heaven. To be great you need to die to self so when you aim to be great in heaven you are really aiming to crucify your fleshly desires and give it all for Him. Only the acts that are motivated by love for His name and glory will remain forever. Love Him, live for Him, and store up as much as you can in heaven. Heaven is real. Once your time here is done you will never again have the opportunity to do it in the same way. Living zealously for the other side is not just for the energetic: it is for the wise.

So You Got It… Can You Keep It?

I have been in what people call "full-time ministry" since 1997. Since then, I have seen people burn up and burn out. There have been many that have fallen into the loving arms of Jesus, received the revelation of His goodness, sprung forth with zeal—wanting to change the world for Christ—and then fizzled out after a short period.

Jesus warned of this in parable of the sower. In this parable, He told us that the Son of Man would come and sow the seed of the kingdom. There would be those people that don't receive this seed because of a hardness of heart. Other people would receive it, but the birds of the air would come and pick it off. Then there would be some people who would receive it with joy, but because of trials and the cares of this life they would wither away after a short period. There were only a few people that would receive the word and then begin to bear fruit for the long haul—a harvest that was thirty-, sixty-, and one-hundred-fold! That is what I am talking about. It is not enough to just receive the revelation of Christ; we want it to bear fruit for the long haul.

Let me put it this way: We don't want to be zealous and bear fruit for only a short period of time; we want to have a deep burning fire in us for the long haul. A zealous fire that does not burn flares up and disappears, but a zealous fire that is aflame remains over time. In order to do this, however, most Jesus lovers will have the opportunity to overcome challenges that come their way—opportunities that seem designed to distinguish zeal.

In my journey, I have had the opportunity presented to me to overcome a few zeal killers head on. Ironically, I have found that these same culprits, once defeated, have served as fuel for the zeal's fire.

There are likely many zeal killers that could be exposed; however, I want to focus on two. They are overcoming the naysayers and overcoming false expectations or false focus. My prayer is that in sharing my challenges I might be able to pass on a key or two that may help you along the way.

Keep the Dream Alive When No One Else Sees It

I remember the season when I began to put form to some dreams God had given me. Prior to this time, I had faithfully served in ways that were palatable in Christian circles and easily understood by those around me. I loved this season. During this time, I served on the worship team, in home groups, in prayer, and with street ministry. My church was awesome, my church family was awesome, and things were great. Then I went to the mission field in Liberia and was infected with a God-dream—a dream that was bigger than expected.

During my prayer times in Liberia, God began to speak to me in a new way. I began to be stirred with vision, not only for my church, community, and city, but for my nation. In this season, I can remember hearing Him whisper to my soul, "Faytene, not only am I going to call you to do things that you have never done before, but I am going to call you to do things that *no one* has ever done before. Get over it. I am looking for those who will boldly go where no Bride has gone before." It was scary and exciting at the same time. I thought everyone around me would be equally excited. I was wrong.

A few years later, I released my first book, *Stand On Guard*. *Stand on Guard* was a compilation of research about the righteous foundations of Canada and a call to our generation to arise and fight for her. Right around the time the book came out, a major moral debate hit Parliament. It was a debate that would seek to reform the age-old Biblical institution of marriage. I knew in my heart that God was asking for more than a book from me; He was asking for authenticity. It was not enough to put the call out there for others to rise up and take the nation—He wanted me to be a part of making it happen. He is always looking for those who will partner with Him to make the word become flesh.

I was zealous, and though I had been in ministry for about seven years at that point, I was still very green, naïve, and somewhat untested—true. Nevertheless, there was a deep burning in my soul that was real. It was a burning that would not stop. I felt God was calling me to raise up a movement of national activism and prayer for the nation. I did not know where it would lead; I just knew I had to do it. Some people around me who I loved and whose opinions I valued did not see it. I can't tell you how hard that was. Just like a young woman who is pregnant with a natural baby *knows* she is pregnant even when no one else can see the baby bump yet, in the same way I *knew* what was alive in me was real even if no one else could see it.

The opposition around me began to grow. There were a few well-intended people that surrounded me and encouraged me to dial down my vision, take a back-seat role, simply doing what I was already doing in ministry.

Everything in my heart wanted to please and be a good girl. I did not want to rock the boat. My honest heart was to hear the council of those around me and make everyone happy. Deeper than that, though, was a desire to obey God. So, I was at a moment of inner conflict. I needed to know if what was in me was really from God or if I indeed needed to heed the discouraging voices around me and forget the dream.

Confused and under pressure, I went back to the Lord and asked Him to test my heart, to take the dream away if it was not from Him. All I wanted was to walk in a way that honored Him. The more I sought the Lord, the more the flame for the nation got brighter. Then I knew the dream was alive: I was not making it up. Moreover, I sensed He was asking me to obey, even in the midst of intense misunderstanding from those around me that I loved and cared for deeply. At that point, in what seemed to be a heavenly extension of God's grace, a few others with whom I had long-term relationship, including my pastors, began to extend support and encouragement to step out with what was burning in my heart. That did not change the fact that the lack of support from others shook my confidence.

The dynamic was a killer. At least it could have been. I found myself at a crossroads. Either I was going to kill the dream in an effort to keep everyone at ease and live the rest of my life wondering what might have happened if I had stepped out, or I was going to do all I could to fortify myself with a humble spirit, honoring those around me that did not see the dream the best I could, and take a risk.

This is honestly one of the finest lines a young leader will have to walk. It is at this point where most either quit or get a bit self-righteous and go forward in bitterness—which, in my assessment, is just as bad. Eventually that bitterness will spring up and defile many.

I was fighting to keep the dream alive and labor with Jesus to bring it about. I desired deeply to simply know that I had done His will. But, even more than this, I needed to know that not only had I done His will, but I had done it **His way**. I don't believe the right thing done in the wrong way is the right thing. It isn't. The call was deeper than just *doing* the assignment. It was deeper than that: I was to look like God while I was being faithful to the call. Jesus is the model. On His way to the cross, in His greatest moment of natural need, Jesus was abandoned by His friends. Not only was He abandoned by His friends, but He called out to the Father and asked Him to forgive the very ones that were crucifying Him stating, "Father forgive them for they do not know what they are doing." This is the call: to be faithful to the assignment, and to do it in full love for those who abandon you, misunderstand you, or even use their own strength to try and crucify you. That is intense! That is love.

If the goal of your life is to be "right," then when you are faced with opposition, your zeal will eventually be strangled out with self-righteousness and bitterness. You will think you are right but in the end you will just be fruitless.

If the goal of you life is to please God, then even when discouragements come you will press into His heart and seek to obey Him, not only in the assignment, but in the way you walk it out. As you embrace this level of humility in the midst of zeal for His kingdom, you will find yourself laying roots deep in your soul that will be very hard to shake in the seasons ahead.

Embrace opposition. Use it to teach you to love. Use it to teach you humility. Use it to test your heart. Sometimes the opposition may have a valid point that needs to be looked at. But once your heart is tested, posture yourself in humility as the virgin Mary did when she said, "Be it done unto me according to your Word." Don't let anything but the voice of your Father lead you. Go for it. Keep the dream alive. Birth the vision. You owe it to the One who put it in you in the first place. He is jealous for His fruit in your life.

Lastly, if you have a discourager or nay-sayer in your life, go out of your way to bless them, love them, and honor them, knowing in your heart that they have been chosen by God to refine you and make you look more like Jesus. What a blessing!

It's All about Perspective: What Is The Point?

The second zeal challenger I have both experienced head-on and rampantly observed in this generation is that of improper expectations or focus. Let's face it: we are a drive-through generation. Compared to the lives of most people around the globe, we have had it exceedingly easy.

Most of us who were born in North America have never experienced war, poverty, or intense religious persecution. Our basic necessities of food, shelter, and water are at our fingertips—so much so that we often don't even think about them. For the most part, even those of us that have had it hard have still had it easy compared to the rest of the earth. This is dangerous. It is dangerous because this atmosphere has the potential to breed a generation of quitters. Why? Because we are so used to having "it" (whatever "it" is) and having it now. We are not used to waiting, working, and doing things simply because they are the right thing to do.

One of my heroes of the faith is Mother Teresa. I am so inspired by her life, zeal, and longevity. She started strong and she finished strong. I have pondered what it was that gave her the strength to continue—every day—in the midst of a massive amount of poverty, death, sickness, and more.

There had to have been days when voices came to her and said, "Why do you keep at it? You are only making a tiny little dent in a nation of millions of people in poverty. So you are helping a few but in the grand scheme of things what are you really accomplishing?" I am sure this voice came from the people around her at times. At other times—especially in the beginning years—I am sure that this voice came from the spirit realm, which ravenously desired her to throw in the towel. I am so glad she didn't. Why didn't she? Where did she get her perseverance in zeal?

I think the answer to that question can be found in one of her most famous quotes: "God has not called me to be successful; He has called me to be faithful." It was all about her perspective. She knew that God did not want her to focus on worldly success but to simply be faithful to Him every moment of every day. We must also catch this revelation.

Mother Teresa's pleasure was not in the attaining of the Nobel Peace Prize or the millions of dollars in donations that eventually began to funnel into her organization. It was not in the masses that came to serve under her leadership in her later years, or in the national or global impact that was eventually to come. Mother Teresa's pleasure was in knowing that she was simply doing what the Lord was asking. It was in faithfulness to her Savior. What is amazing about her testimony is that though her focus was not worldly success, she was arguably one of the most successful women of the past century. Should we be surprised? Jesus told us this would happen. He said, "Seek first the kingdom and His righteousness, and all these things will be given to you as well" (Matthew 6:13, NIV).

The reason Mother Teresa did not quit when the going got tough was because she had her focus in the right place. Not only did she have her perspective in the right place, but she also had a proper expectation. She knew that the Lord Himself promised persecution and suffering for those that truly picked up their cross and followed Him. She was not surprised by it; therefore, it did not discourage her. She saw times of suffering for Christ as a joy to walk through for Him. Her faithfulness through tough times released a deep inner intimacy with Jesus that cannot be attained in any other way. The apostle Paul called it the fellowship of His sufferings.

For those who truly pick up their cross and follow Him, there is a depth of union and intimacy released with Him that is beyond words. I remember tasting this truth clearly while on the mission field in Liberia. There were days where the heat was so intense that I hardly remembered what it was to be cool. I had not showered in months (because we did not have a shower), I had not seen my family in months, my primary food staple had been rice, there was an aggressive snake nest outside the front door of the compound I was staying in, and malaria-infested mosquitoes were inside my room. I could go on and on. It was not the Hilton, but, ironically, I was more alive there than I had ever been my life.

When I returned home, people would say to me, "It must have been so hard. Was it?" I would respond honestly and say, "No. It wasn't hard at all. There is nothing more amazing than being in the center of God's will. No matter how uncomfortable or dangerous it is, He always gives you grace to do what He has asked you to do."

It is true; we can do all things through Christ who strengthens us. I want to take this a tad deeper though. God is looking for friends not just slaves. He is looking for those that will be willing to put their hand in His and go to the toughest, most intense, most uncomfortable regions of the earth with Him to chase down the people that His heart is burning for. He is looking for those that are not interested in the results as their primary focus; they simply want to be with Him. There is a wild place of intimacy with Jesus for those who, in zealous love for Him, give it their all and live this way.

I call it the *God-war bond*. You know what I mean? It is that special bond that is formed when you experience war or an intense battle with someone at your side. You see this dynamic with those who have served in the army or with high-level athletes in team sports. There is a bond, an intimacy that is deeper than words. Only those that have been on the battlefield understand.

Some of my most intimate times with Jesus have been on the battlefield. I will never forget the day in Liberia when I saw Him move heaven and earth, arrange schedules, lead by word of knowledge, give favor, and give finances, all to save a couple of orphans. I felt His pleasure that day in an extreme way. Not only did I feel His pleasure, I fell so in love with Him as I saw His mercy and compassion in such a tangible way. The result: lives were saved and a war bond was secured. I will never be the same. Those who quit early never get to taste the depth of intimacy that comes from the fellowship of His sufferings on the frontlines of battle.

I dare to you to feel what He feels in the uncomfortable zones of life that require great perseverance and faithfulness. Dare to live with your focus on faithfulness instead of anything else. I promise you, if you do, it will give you an inner zeal that will survive the test of time. True burners live for His pleasure and His pleasure alone. It is their fuel. This is why their zeal never runs out.

How many potential champions quit a little too early because their focus was not on the simplicity of faithfulness? How many allowed discouragement or failure to set up camp in their soul in the midst of desert seasons or small beginnings? These people quit because they lost sight of this one thing: God has called us to be faithful; the rest is up to Him.

I once heard a great prophetic teacher of our time, Rick Joyner, say that there is no success without sacrifice. If you sacrifice without apparent success, it is because someone will succeed after you because of your labors. If you have success without sacrifice, it is because someone sacrificed before you.

I would like to add that the greater reward goes to the one who gave the most, not to the one who reaped the most. Oh what revelation bliss! Nothing done in faithfulness to the Lord is ever wasted—ever. This is so freeing. It takes all performance pressure off and puts our focus back in the right place. The enemy of zeal would have us focus on results, numbers, towers, or buildings. God is the true source of zeal and He simply says, "Seek my kingdom and you get it all."

Run Your Race and Burn for Him

It is such an honor to be a person of God's zeal. As we discussed at the opening of this chapter, Jesus is the ultimate man of zeal. He is the originator of it. We get it from Him through impartation and through revelation—whether a revelation of eternity, His ways, or His desires burning in our soul as an expression of our connection to Him. Our zeal may be challenged, indeed, but if grounded in faithful devotion to Him, it cannot easily be defeated.

When we persevere in this life of zeal we reveal a part of who He is to our generation. What an amazing privilege. I don't know about you but I deeply want to reveal Him to those around me, and He is a man of zeal. Therefore a lazy, apathetic, dreamless Christian does not reveal God. Be zealous. Always.

For those who don't have zeal yet, the challenge is to get it. Let's continue to receive the impartation of His zealous nature by faith. Ask for revelation that will cause zeal to erupt like a burning inferno in your soul.

For those that have zeal, the challenge is to keep it and to keep it pure. The zeal that lasts the test of time and bears great fruit is not loud, it is deep—motivated out of a deep desire to simply do whatever He asks. Oh how I hunger to be a friend of God and to run with a generation of His friends in the earth. Friends behave out of loyalty and love, not duty or dry servitude. When this is your motivation you will never quit: you can't. True friendships last a lifetime. True friends are with you to the end. Let's labor to be His zealous friends all the way to the end—no matter what the cost.

I believe that you are a person who loves Jesus or wants to love Jesus, or you would not be reading these words now. I pray that God would bless you with His holy zeal right now. Pray this with me:

> Jesus, I thank You that You are the author of zeal. It comes from You. Live Your zeal through my life. Let it burn in my soul with unquenchable fire. Grant me the revelation I need to live a zealous life for You. Kill the unholy ambition. Ignite the God dream. Give me the courage to step out and the faithfulness to finish to the end. I realize souls are at stake and that this is what You came for. As Your friend I want to give You what You are after. Jesus, at the end of it all, let it be said of me that I was a friend of God—zealous for Your honor and Your pleasure. I want to live for You, Jesus. I want to be zealous for You and with You—to the end.

About the Author

Faytene Grasseschi was radically saved in 1995 and began in full time Christian ministry in 1997 on the inner city streets of Vancouver where she served the urban poor and drug addicted. In 2000 she transitioned to overseas missions in the war-torn nation of Libera. There she had the joy of picking up orphans one at a time and establishing a mercy ministry to care for their needs. In 2003 Faytene began to receive the call of God to raise up a movement of national revival and reformation in her home nation of Canada. She returned to Canada, wrote her first book, which became a national bestseller, and launched TheCRY Movement and MY Canada Association. These national movements have mobilized thousands of believers in prayer and national activism. During this period the nation of Canada has seen dramatic shifts of which this movement has been an active part. As of 2011 Faytene is happily married to Robert Grasseschi and they have continued in missions, revivalism, and activism both in Canada and internationally. Find out more at www.robertjohnandfaytene.com. There you will find links to all their ministry sites.

Chapter 7

Abiding in the Fullness of God

Morgan Perry

It was a damp, quiet morning when we left the hostel to work for the day at an orphanage in Chang Mia, Thailand. It was a morning like most—bars were cleaning up from the night before and countless tuk-tuks whizzed by with drivers yelling, "You want ride?" My Youth With A Mission (YWAM) outreach team was naturally quiet because no one had his or her morning coffee yet. We soon came around the corner to the bar where we had ministered to young prostitutes the night before.

I thought about what happened the previous night. I had been having a conversation with one of the girls when, in mid-sentence, a western man around my father's age interrupted us, shamelessly agreed on a price, and took her upstairs to have sex. These girls would open up to me about their lives, but at the blink of an eye, turn on their seductive act as soon as men came around the corner. Did they want to be there? Did they enjoy selling their bodies for sex? All of these questions flooded my mind when we came around the corner and saw the repugnant bar in the daylight.

What I saw next changed my life forever. As we approached the bar, I saw a girl passed out against the wall of the building. She was almost completely naked and had been drugged and raped numerous times. The evidence was on the sidewalk.

Paralyzed by fear, I stood there looking at her as my outreach leader abruptly took off her jacket, covered the girl, and shouted, "Someone call an anti-trafficking organization!"

That was the first time I heard the term "sex trafficking." This was in 2006, and I was eighteen years old. That night I prayed to the Lord from the rooftop of the hostel that He would use me in any way to rescue and restore these women.

I would soon discover that according to the Department of State Trafficking in Persons (TIP) report, there are an estimated twenty-seven million people enslaved as bonded laborers and prostitutes worldwide. There are more slaves in the world today than at any other point in history: 80 percent of whom are women and girls. Human trafficking is the world's second largest and fastest growing criminal industry, generating $32 billion dollars annually.

In the United States alone there are an estimated 100,000 to 300,000 children at risk of being sex trafficked every year. That is enough children to fill three or four NFL football stadiums. The average age of entry into prostitution in America is twelve to thirteen years old. It is estimated that these children are forced to service a minimum of five customers per day. So, taking the lowest estimate of 100,000 children servicing five customers per day, that would be at least a half million rapes of children, per day, in America.

Back in 2006, I had no idea how much the girl on the street and my prayer on the rooftop would change the course of my life. Seven years later, I'm still fighting this injustice as a full-time missionary with YWAM. I've had the privilege of partnering with many to help rescue girls who have been trafficked, see traffickers and sex offenders prosecuted, and restoration homes built for survivors all over the world. After I said yes to God, He took me on a journey to radically increase my faith, strengthen my biblical foundation, and shape who I am today. It seems, however, that His primary goal was to teach me how to truly abide in His fullness.

In Philippians 3:2–14, the apostle Paul wrote with great zeal that whatever gain he had on his own, he counted as *rubbish* compared to the surpassing worth of gaining, knowing, and being found in Christ. He went on to say that he pressed on toward that goal, forgetting what lies behind, for the prize of the upward call of God in Christ Jesus. In verse 15 he wrote, "Let those of us who are mature think this way, and if any of you think otherwise, God will reveal that also to you" (ESV).

We have seen evidence that a new revival and missions movement is taking place all over the world today. Hundreds of thousands of people are saying "Yes!" to the radical call of God on their lives. But what happens after the initial "mountain-top" experience when you first hear God calling you in a certain direction? What happens when things get tough? How do you maintain zeal for the long haul?

Whether you're called to end abortion, plant houses of prayer, or reach millions with the Gospel, it is true for everyone that apart from God we cannot maintain zeal. No matter how great the cause, without abiding in the fullness of God we will all eventually run out of steam.

Knowing and Hearing the Voice of God

Communicating with God is one of the most intimate ways to increase our friendship and fullness in Him. When we know we are directly communicating with our heavenly Father, we can't help but become revived! In Psalm 63, David wrote about his soul thirsting and being fully satisfied in God. He said in verse 3, "Experiencing your loyal love is better than life itself, my lips praise you" (ESV).

How can we hear God speak in our lives if we do not wait to hear His voice? How can we hear His voice if we do not know what He sounds like, and if we do not have faith to believe that He desires to communicate with us?

There is an undeniable theme throughout Scripture that the Lord created us to be in constant communication with Him. From Genesis to Revelation there are countless examples of the Lord choosing to communicate directly with His people. God speaks to, commands, commissions, rebukes, comforts, performs miracles for, makes covenants with, encourages, heals, listens to, answers, and fights for His children.

God is intentional in His desire to communicate. We can see examples of this throughout the Bible. God expressed His desire to communicate when He walked and talked with Adam and Eve in the garden and made covenants with Noah and Abraham. We can see God communicating when He gave prophetic dreams to Jacob, Joseph, Abimelek, Solomon, and Pilate's wife. He sent angels to speak with Moses, Gideon, and Mary, and He answered the cries of the prophets, Job, David, and many other people in

Scripture and through Christian history. God is so eager to communicate with us that He even sent His own son, Jesus, to live on earth and die on the cross for our sins.

Jesus communicates with us too. After His resurrection, He appeared to Mary of Bethany, the disciples, and even the apostle Paul. He gave us the Holy Spirit to lead us into all truth and help us have discernment for His Word. The Lord communicates with His creation in countless ways. However, we seem to lose sight of this truth nowadays within the Body of Christ. We pray routine laundry lists of requests to the Lord, but do not expect Him to respond. We ask Him for direction, yet our hearts are lacking in faith that He is going to answer.

After spending six years as a slave in Ireland, a young Christian man heard a voice telling him it would soon be time for him to escape and go home, and that a ship would be waiting for him. This young man responded in faith by fleeing his master and boarding an available ship back to his home in Roman-occupied Britain. A few years after being there, when he was in his early twenties, he had a vision of Irish people crying out to him saying "We appeal to you, holy servant boy, to come and walk among us."[2] He took that as a word from the Lord that he was to return to Ireland as a free man to spread the Gospel.

What this young man could not have predicted was that shortly after he returned to Ireland, the Rhine River froze over allowing the barbarians to cross over from Ancient Germany into Roman territory. Once they arrived in Rome, they burned the city, wiping out centuries of learning and civilization, including Scripture. However, this young man had taken manuscripts of the Gospel back to Ireland with him and the Word of God was spreading.

Motivated by the Gospel, the Irish monks considered it their Christian duty to copy all the books in danger of being lost as the Roman Empire was being sacked. The Irish monks eventually traveled to fallen Rome with books tied to their belts, established monasteries, and saved Western Civilization for all of us. If it were not for this young man knowing the voice of God in his life and choosing to respond in faith, we would not have the Bible today. This young man became known as the Apostle of Ireland, or more commonly known as St. Patrick.

St. Patrick is just one of thousands of examples in church history of people who knew and responded to the voice of God in their lives. If we know God and are in constant communion with Him, then—and only then—are we able to make Him effectively known to others. God desires to be in close relationship with all of His children, not just a select few people (1 Timothy 2:1–4). Some of the ways He communicates are through Scripture, dreams, visions, prophecy, and seasons of prayer, worship and fasting. One of the best ways to maintain zeal is by knowing that you are hearing God speak in your life.

Getting a Clear Vision

Hearing from God also helps us get a clear and defined vision. One of the most profound ways I've heard the voice of God in my life was in the spring of 2007, while I was studying the Bible in Switzerland. This was a year after my time in Thailand. I was doing my homework one afternoon in a field overlooking the Alps, when I suddenly had a vision. It seemed like a daydream at first, but because the picture was so vivid I decided to write it down.

In this vision, I saw a stadium full of people. Everyone in the stadium was watching a film on a big screen. I could tell by the expressions on their faces that the film was exposing a serious injustice. Once the film was finished, I walked out on the stage with a band, and we helped lead them into a time of response to the film. At first, the stadium was filled with deep emotion as people wept in repentance before the Lord.

Eventually, the Spirit in the stadium shifted to that of joy and revival as people danced before the Lord. The verse that God gave me for the vision was Jeremiah 20:9 where Jeremiah said,

> Then I said, "I will not make mention of Him, nor speak anymore in His name." But His word was in my heart like a burning fire shut up in my bones; I was weary of holding it back, but I could not. (NKJV)

The interpretation I had for the vision was that the Lord was going to give our generation assignments that would burn on our hearts like fire shut up in our bones. We would be compelled to communicate the message to the masses. He was going to break our hearts for what was breaking His. I felt that the Lord wanted to utilize the existing justice trend within our generation to not only continue humanitarian efforts, but to primarily expose injustice as a tool to spark repentance, revival, and reformation in society.

After seeing this vision, I ran back to the YWAM campus and called my sister, Megan. She was at Hillsong College in Australia studying worship leading at the time. I told her about the vision and told her that I felt strongly that God was going to give us His heart for an issue, and that we were going to use media to communicate it. I also told her that I felt like we would tour around America, and perhaps the world, facilitating events that would spark revival and reformation.

Several months later I went to visit her in Australia. As soon as I landed, she took me to the chapel service at Hillsong. There was a guest speaker from New Zealand speaking that evening. When he was done preaching, he told the group that he felt strongly that the Lord wanted him to prophesy over three people. He briefly explained God's heart in communicating through prophecy, and then he looked straight to the back of the room and said, "You in the red shirt, come forward."

I nervously glanced down in an effort to remember what I was wearing and it was, in fact, a red shirt. I looked at him and pointed to myself questionably and he confirmed, so I walked to the front. The Lord used a man who I had never met before to confirm the vision that He gave me while doing my homework in a field in Switzerland. The Lord not only confirmed the vision, but also encouraged me, as a nineteen-year old, not to doubt Him, but to trust Him. The Lord instructed me to be tenacious, have great faith, and to know my identity in Him alone. After he finished speaking, I walked back to the last row where Megan was and we were both overwhelmed with emotion.

How could we doubt the Lord? Why were we so surprised that He was communicating so clearly to us? Five years later, God would use me to produce a documentary about child sex trafficking in America and the modern-day abolitionist movement that is fighting to stop it called *Sex+Money: A National Search for Human Worth*. Then in August 2011, Megan and I, along with thirteen other radical missionaries, jumped into a forty-two-foot tour bus and traveled to all fifty states and Canada to screen the film and facilitate revival-type meetings. The vision that God showed me in Switzerland had become a reality.

One of the events that stood out was our screening at Liberty University when over eight hundred students came out to watch the film. When the film was finished, the worship team and I went on stage and shared a message about raising our personal standards to match those of Christ. I shared about the Body of Christ's direct contribution to driving the demand for child sex trafficking in America through pornography. According to the Barna Group, 50 percent of Christian men and 30 percent of Christian women look at porn. When the students at Liberty realized that their individual freedom and choices to engage in sinful behavior were driving someone else's slavery, repentance hit the room.

All of a sudden, our prayer teams were bombarded by students coming forward for prayer. They repented and received healing from backgrounds of sexual abuse, use of pornography, and even passivity when it came to caring for those in great need, among other things. After prayer, there was a shift in the room to that of joy-filled relief and worship. It was truly a miraculous evening!

After we left Liberty University and moved on to the next state, we continued to hear reports weeks later. Students were voluntarily going to their resident assistants (RAs) to hand in their pornography, cigarettes, and drugs. They told their RAs that they didn't want to continue living in their sinful lifestyles anymore. Praise the Lord!

Knowing that you have heard clearly from the Lord and then seeing glimpses of His great work is a sure way to maintain zeal. However, one of the greatest challenges is maintaining the zeal in the seemingly unfruitful or trying seasons.

Overcoming Obstacles and Opposition

How do you maintain zeal even if you do not see fruit for several months or even years? Seasons of obstacles and opposition can be the most significant times in our lives to find fullness in God. Learning to navigate through hard seasons with the

Lord have been the most rewarding experiences of my life. I had the vision in the field in Switzerland in 2007, but didn't hit the road with a completed documentary until 2011. The venues on our tour were not stadiums full of thousands of people like I saw in the vision, but rather, auditoriums and sanctuaries filled with a few, and on occasion hundreds, of people. The lowest attended screening during our fifty-state tour was in Vermont where only two people came, both of whom we already knew.

I can still remember the feelings of doubt and anxiety right before we started shooting the documentary in September 2009. I was twenty-one years old at the time and had very limited prior experience in film production. The film crew was primarily made up of friends from film school. But the rest of the crew were passionate prayer warriors and missionaries with YWAM. Everyone had booked their flights and production was scheduled to start in only a few weeks, yet at that point I had been unsuccessful in raising any of the projected $500,000 budget.

A few weeks before everyone's arrival, I finally hit the wall. I confessed to my close friend and right-hand producer, Autumn, that I had lost all hope that the film was ever going to happen. I randomly decided to voice that concern to one of our interns as well. She suggested that I call her father, Scott. He asked me to practice my pitch for the film with him and his initial feedback was, "Only articulate your vision like that if you're trying to raise money from your grandparents."

The pressure was on, and I was overwhelmingly aware of my inability. I had already thought of ways to entertain the film crew for a week before sending them all home in defeat. Scott eventually suggested that we jump on a conference call with one of his friends to see if this man would be interested in giving. Our biggest need at that point was $20,000 to be able to leave the drive-way and start the project. Nearly a week before the production started, I finally got on a conference call with Scott and his friend. I spent the entire morning in desperate intercession and wrote my entire pitch out word for word. With a shaky and nervous voice, I shared our vision with this man and within twenty minutes on the conference call he generously donated the first $20,000 that we needed to hit the road!

I was so caught off guard that when he said he wanted to give, I said, "Really?" Thankfully he chuckled and said, "For future reference, never sound surprised when a donor decides to invest in your project." Two years later, this generous man said to our team, "You should be very proud of how you are investing your lives. If more people lived like you do, the glory of God would be apparent to everyone."

Over the next two years, God provided over $1.2 million in cash, donated services, and gifts in kind for our team to produce the documentary and embark on a nationwide distribution tour through all fifty states and Canada.

God delights in using very ordinary people to do extraordinary things because it points back to God and brings Him glory. The best way to build trust and increase faith in your walk with the Lord is by chasing after the impossible so God can *make* it possible! Oftentimes the greatest ability that a Christian can possess is to simply be available. Through the hard and seemingly insignificant seasons of ministry, it is imperative to remember that God can do what you cannot do. Whatever you can do, it is only because He has given you the grace to do it.

A Biblical Perspective on Burnout

There are countless examples throughout Scripture of great men and women doubting their call from the beginning and losing their zeal during hard seasons. Moses walked and communed with God like no other person recorded in the Old Testament scriptures. Moses was probably one of the greatest men of God to have ever lived. The words that God used to describe Moses could not be more highly esteemed. In Numbers 12:6–8, the Lord says,

> Listen to my words: "When there is a prophet among you, I, the Lord, reveal myself to them in visions, I speak to them in dreams. But this is not true of my servant Moses; he is faithful in all my house. With him I speak face to face, clearly and not in riddles; he sees the form of the Lord. Why then were you not afraid to speak against my servant Moses?" (NIV)

Yet even Moses, who walked in such communion with the Lord, still burned out while in the wilderness. In Numbers 11:11–15, Moses said,

> If this is how you are going to treat me, please go ahead and kill me—if I have found favor in your eyes—and do not let me face my own ruin. (NIV)

Other great men including Elijah, Job, and Jonah also cried out to the Lord to be killed in the hardest seasons of their ministries. I find it comforting to know that biblical heroes hit the wall, too. Often their burnouts were far more dramatic than mine because their missions and callings were significantly more demanding than mine as well. It's humbling and inspiring to read how much persecution the prophets endured or how many years Noah labored over building a giant ark in the middle of a drought in front of all of his skeptical friends and family. The most inspiring aspect of observing these biblical heroes is seeing how God responded to each of their prayers according to what they *actually* needed.

Elijah, Job, Jonah, and Moses cried out for God to take their lives. Isaiah, Habbakuk, and David (among many others) questioned whether or not God had abandoned them in their situation. However, when Moses cried out for the Lord to take his life, instead of God answering that prayer, God gave Moses seventy men to help him continue in his leadership. When Elijah said he would rather die than move forward, God put him into a deep sleep, woke him up, and fed him, and then put him back to sleep again.

When hard seasons of ministry come, we need to pray that the Lord provides what we need according to His will and specifically ask for Him to help us maintain zeal. Romans 8:26–28 instructs us:

> In the same way, the Spirit helps us in our weakness. We do not know what we ought to pray for, but the Spirit himself intercedes for us through wordless groans. And he who searches our hearts knows the mind of the Spirit, because the Spirit intercedes for God's people in accordance with the will of God. And we know that in all things God works for the good of those who love him, who have been called according to his purpose. (NIV)

It's reassuring to know that great men and women of God burnout, but it is more comforting to know that *God is always faithful.* What these biblical heroes also have in common is that after they questioned the Lord and God responded, they followed through with their mission wholeheartedly—even to the point of martyrdom. One of the greatest struggles for our generation is that we have a microwave mindset: we want instant results. We have to keep in mind that the awesome biblical and historical heroes we all admire labored for decades and sacrificed extraordinarily to be faithful in what God called them to do. The longer we stick with what God has called us to do, the greater our relationship with Him will become.

Focusing on Jesus: Primary Source of Zeal

Colossians 1:19 says that "God in all his fullness was pleased to live in Christ" (NLT). It is always helpful to observe biblical heroes, but nothing is more inspiring than observing the life and sacrifice of Jesus Christ. Even Jesus questioned whether or not He could bear what was ahead when He fell on His face in prayer and said, "My Father, if it be possible, let this cup pass from me."

However, Christ set the standard for us in trusting God the Father with our lives when He finished the prayer with: "Nevertheless, not as I will, but as you will" (Matthew 26:39, ESV).

Focusing on Christ and His humble and perfect leadership has always been my primary source of maintaining zeal in ministry. Jesus knew how much it was going to cost for Him to follow through with what God was calling Him to do, and yet He still chose to do it. Jesus also knew that His death was going to be atonement for our sins against God.

In my ministry, I fight for the lives of women and children who are being raped for profit because they deserve justice. Others defend the life of the unborn because they deserve the right to live. However, Jesus did not die on the cross for the innocent, but for the guilty. Christ knew that His sacrifice was the only way we could still have access to the Father despite our wretched sinful nature. Though we were undeserving, Christ gave up His life for us.

That is the ultimate sacrifice. I've noticed that a primary way people lose zeal in what they are doing is by complaining and over-focusing on the negative. Whenever I'm having a day or a season where every sacrifice I'm making to serve the Lord seems like the greatest sacrifice of all time, I remember what Christ did for me. Compared to Christ, our attitudes towards sacrificing for ministry become "This is the least I can do."

I have meditated on John 15–17 for years and will continue to meditate on it for the rest of my life. I cannot read those chapters without having the zeal of the Lord rekindled in my heart. Of course, the greatest revivalist field manual is the *entire* Bible, but I would especially recommend those chapters as a solid prescription for reviving hearts and maintaining zeal.

Sustaining Zeal through Abiding in Him

John chapters 15–17 are instructions for how to abide in Him to maintain zeal. These chapters are foundational in pursuing fullness in God. By abiding in Him, we are giving Him full authority, leadership, and responsibility to do several things in our lives.

First, we are giving Him the authority to be the Gardener who has full permission to prune our lives in order to produce the kind of fruit that lasts and brings Him glory. We are entrusting our lives with His leadership to bear eternal fruit no matter the cost. That is the only kind of fruit that matters!

Second, we are positioning ourselves to have His joy—a joy that is made *complete*. What a profound and wonderful promise the Lord makes when we abide in Him! His joy will be in us and it will be complete!

Third, by abiding in Him we come to realize that He said "I love you" to each of us more profoundly than we will ever experience on this side of heaven. Christ's sacrifice for us emphasizes His very words that we did not choose Him, but He chose us and is calling us His friends! We are loved, chosen, and befriended by our Lord Jesus Christ!

Jesus said in John 15:13–17 (NIV):

> "My command is this: Love each other as I have loved you. Greater love has no one than this: to lay down one's life for one's friends. You are my friends if you do what I command. I no longer call you servants, because a servant does not know his master's business. Instead, I have called you friends, for everything that I learned from my Father I have made known to you. You did not choose me, but I chose you and appointed you so that you might go and bear fruit—fruit that will last—and so that whatever you ask in my name the Father will give you. This is my command: Love each other."

Mother Teresa once said, "Work without love is slavery." A quick way to burnout or lose zeal is by feeling like you are doing ministry as a *slave* of God, instead of a *friend* of God. Our love for God has to be the driving force behind why we do what we do. Once we start viewing sacrifice as an opportunity to worship God, we become worshipers and adorers, not just doers.

John 15:18–25 tells us what our perspective should be when facing persecution. The first thing Christ highlights is that no matter how severe the persecution is, the truth still remains that "the world hated Him first." Christ goes on to explain that the reason we face persecution and difficulty in ministry is because "we are not of this world," but instead we are a threat to the enemy. So, if we are facing persecution we should take that as a good sign because it means we are effectively "not of this world."

Satan would not waste his time trying to derail you if you weren't being effective in advancing the kingdom of God. Count warfare as a credential on the mission field! Don't let spiritual warfare discourage you, but instead, praise the Lord that He will triumph over the evil and praise Him for giving you an effective ministry!

John 15:26–27 and 16:13 explain the great ministry of the Holy Spirit to help give us discernment and lead us into all truth: not some truth, but *all* truth. The final point I want to highlight from these three chapters is in John 17:6–26 when Jesus prays for the disciples and for all believers.

We should pray this over ourselves regularly. It's a reminder that Christ is to be glorified, and that He is our great intercessor sitting at the right hand of God. He contends for our breakthrough in advancing His kingdom on earth as it is in heaven.

Understanding His Grace is Sufficient, No Matter the Circumstance

> My grace is sufficient for you, for my power is made perfect in weakness. —2 Corinthians 2:9, NIV

Someone who has modeled this lifestyle for me and personally inspired me to say yes to God is my grandfather, Pastor Dick Woodward. In the late 1970s, my grandfather had a vision from the Lord about creating a Bible study program that would make "the whole Word available to the whole world."

After the Lord gave my grandfather this vision, he thought his ministry was about to increase exponentially. He had already planted two rapidly growing churches in Virginia and was a devoted husband and father of five. However, shortly after receiving the vision, he was diagnosed with a rare degenerative disease of the spinal cord that slowly and steadily left him a bed-ridden quadriplegic. Instead of giving up and falling into depression, my grandfather pressed into the Lord for His friendship, perspective, and radical provision. He didn't pursue these things on principle, but rather, he pursued fullness in God because his life depended on it.

The Lord not only provided him with perspective and joy despite his circumstances, but He also encouraged my grandfather to keep moving forward with the vision of making the whole Word available for the whole word. Eventually, he was given a voice-activated computer, and through the inspiration of the Holy Spirit, he completed the Mini Bible College (MBC), which is a practical, easy-to-understand, systematic, and expository survey of the scriptures.

Today, the MBC has been translated into over thirty languages and is being used by International Cooperating Ministries (ICM) and Iris Ministries for church planting all over the world. The MBC has been the foundational teaching tool that has helped plant over four thousand churches with twenty thousand sister churches in over sixty countries through ICM. It is also being used in over ten thousand churches worldwide through Iris Ministries. ICM's vision is to equip one million evangelists worldwide by 2020 through over fifty thousand church plants.

Revival is sweeping the nations and millions of people are receiving the Gospel from a paralyzed man lying on a bed in Virginia who can't even scratch his own nose. In addition, my grandfather has chronic muscular and bone pain from lying in the same position everyday. If you ask my grandfather if he's surprised by how the Lord is using him despite his circumstances, his most common response is: "Well, if the Lord can speak through a donkey like He did in Numbers 22:28, then I guess he can speak through me too."

I told my grandfather that I was working on this chapter and asked him how he maintains zeal in his life. He responded, "First you believe, then you obey, and then you rely on God's grace to keep you going." He told a story of a man who visited him several years ago who had been listening to his teachings for a long time. When he walked in the room and saw my grandfather's condition the man said, "Dick, I have no idea how you are able to stay so joyful. If I were in your shape, I would never be able to handle it."

My grandfather responded, "You're right. You're looking at me and trying to imagine yourself in a situation that God has not given you grace for; therefore, you feel you would not be able to handle it. However, if I were you looking at me, I wouldn't be able to handle it either. If you were given my limitations and you asked God daily to measure out His grace according to what you need, then you would be able to handle it." My grandfather responded by quoting 2 Corinthians 9:8 (NIV):

> And God is able to bless you abundantly, so that in all things at all times, having all that you need, you will abound in every good work.

He emphasized *all* and *every* in the verse. He made the point that even though his body has limitations, there are no limits to that verse. He said that when most people read that verse they think God over-sold the product of grace. However, the reality is that God didn't oversell the product; we simply don't know how to access it.

The way to access extraordinary grace is by believing and obeying. He said the key to salvation is *believing* and the key to sanctification (becoming holy) is *obeying*. In John 3, Nicodemus asked Jesus *how* someone can be born again and Jesus said, "Whoever *believes* in Him will not perish but have eternal life" (emphasis mine). When pursuing sanctification and maintaining zeal after salvation, the key is to *obey*. Acts 5:32 says that the Holy Spirit is given to those who obey the Lord. We are given the Holy Spirit when we obey because that's when we need the Spirit the most.

Simply Follow Jesus

Matthew 4:19 records that Jesus made a covenant with His followers when He said, "Follow me—and I will make you fishers of men" (ESV). A covenant means there's God's part, and then our part. Jesus said that if we follow Him, then He will make us fishers of men. We aren't equipped until we follow. And God is the one who does the equipping, not us. We simply have to be obedient in following Him wherever He leads and calls us.

In closing, let's pray together:

> Lord Jesus, thank You for Your leadership! Thank You for Your friendship! Thank You for being so *worthy* of being followed and so *worthy* of being praised! Our main prayer is that we may find fullness in You, Lord. We want to hear from You. Please teach us how to hear Your voice in our lives and how to have faith to follow You wherever You are leading us. We submit our dreams and visions to Your *perfect* leadership. God, we ask for You to be the Gardener. Please prune our ministries and hearts to produce eternal fruit that brings You ALL the glory. We ask for Your

grace and zeal to sustain us in the mission. We ask for zeal that comes through *knowing You* and being in *deep friendship with You*. Help us to know You more, God! Help us to make You known to others. Sync our hearts, attitudes, and actions to Yours! Humble us. Help us overcome burnout and desires to quit because of obstacles and opposition. Help us to be patient. Your timing is *perfect* Lord, and we trust You! Help us to overcome our microwave mentalities; we want to be in this for the long haul! Help us to keep the first thing *first* (Matthew 22:37–39).

Our final prayer is Ephesians 3:16–21 (NIV):

I pray that out of His glorious riches He may strengthen you with power through His Spirit in your inner being, so that Christ may dwell in your hearts through faith. And I pray that you, being rooted and established in love, may have power, together with all the Lord's holy people, to grasp how wide and long and high and deep is the love of Christ, and to know this love that surpasses knowledge—that you may be filled to the measure of all the fullness of God. Now to Him who is able to do immeasurably more than all we ask or imagine, according to His power that is at work within us, to Him be glory in the church and in Christ Jesus throughout all generations, for ever and ever! Amen.

About the Author:

Morgan Perry has been a media missionary with Youth With A Mission (YWAM) since 2006. She is the Executive Producer/

Producer of the documentary and national campaign *Sex+Money: A National Search for Human Worth* (released in 2011). Morgan studied Mass Media in nearly thirty countries through the University of the Nations (U of N), which is a training branch of YWAM. The Lord gripped Morgan's heart for combating sex trafficking after she saw a young prostitute left for dead on the streets of Thailand in 2006. She was compelled to shed light on this atrocity by co-writing a book on international human trafficking. While researching to write the book, she was shocked to discover the same injustice was happening in America. As a result, she produced the *Sex+Money* documentary and launched a national campaign to screen the film in all fifty states and Canada. In 2012, she received a Certificate of Recognition for her work in combating sex trafficking from the United States Department of Justice, Office of Justice Programs and the Office of Juvenile Justice and Delinquency Prevention. As a media-missionary, Morgan feels called to tell stories that will positively impact society and ones that desperately need to be told. Connect with Morgan at www.sexandmoneyfilm.com or www.kmediaproductions.com.

Chapter 8

Hope for Every Nation

Andrew York

*May God be gracious to us and bless us
and make His face to shine upon us,
that Your way may be known on earth,
Your saving power among all nations.*
—Psalm 67:1–2, ESV

During the summer of 2010, Bob Hartley told our Youth With A Mission (YWAM) Awaken community that we were to be "hope reformers." Later, he also told me that I would personally be given a "song for Korea." That night, I was so excited to get to my room to try to compose a song. I tried for hours to write something but I got nothing.

The night of December 17, 2011, felt no different than any other night in my little room in Kona, Hawaii, except that my friend Michael was sleeping on the futon. As I began to drift asleep, I said a prayer asking for God's presence to fill the room and to grant us dreams and visions in the night—it's sort of become my bedtime ritual. As our spirits never sleep, the night hours are prime for inviting the Holy Spirit to come encounter us.

The next thing I knew, I was standing in the presence of God. I felt that I was before the Lord. I was unable to see Him, but I was very aware of His nearness. The next thing I remember was a box placed before me. The box was so large that I had to reach down to retrieve the gift inside. I pulled out a message that said, "Behold, I am doing something new." While I was reading, an emotion began to bubble up within my spirit. Before I had time to figure out what was happening, like a cup overflowing, I began to make a sound. It felt like something, or someone, was singing through me. I remember feeling awe, fear, and excitement. I began to weep as I felt the release of this song that was now flowing through me. The experience was slightly terrifying. Yet, as I felt a gamut of emotions, the overwhelming sense was that of *hope*.

"Bro! Are you okay?" My startled roommate woke me up.

"Yes, I think so." I shook the sleep off and I realized that there were tears in my eyes. "Was I singing?" I asked.

"You were making a noise!" (I guess Michael didn't like my song very much.) There we both sat in the darkness not really sure what to do, but definitely feeling the weightiness that something was happening in that room.

I looked at the clock. It was 2:17 a.m. At that moment, I felt the LORD say, "Isaiah 2:17." I looked up the verse in my Bible (ESV). It says,

And the haughtiness of man shall be humbled, and the lofty pride of men shall be brought low, and the LORD alone will be exalted in that day.

I remember lying back down, a little uncertain what was happening, unable to shake the thought that God was indeed doing "something new."

The next morning, December 18, I went about my day, still a little puzzled by the previous night's activity. Three hours later, I received a call from a friend asking, "Have you heard the news about North Korea?" My friend told me that the leader of North Korea, Kim Jung II, had just passed away. *What in the world?* I thought to myself. I found Michael later in the day, and we stood in awe of how God had very purposefully visited us that night to declare that something new was happening.

It wasn't long after that North Korea began testing nuclear weapons. Many people have proclaimed that North Korea and its people are hopeless. Some say it's an evil empire. As I consider my experience, I am more and more convinced that my dream was an actual encounter with God. He wanted to bring me into a greater awareness of a heavenly reality—an awareness where I recognize my spiritual place of standing before His throne, where He invites me to see the way He sees things, and where I see Him as victoriously reigning. Had I not been given this divine perspective, my soul would have easily caved to discouragement in the days following the dream.

God filled me with a substance of hope. And now I trumpet the sound of hope over this "hopeless" communist nation. Hope is a sound that pierces the silence of despair and awakens the soul to the reality of Christ's light in the darkest hours. There's nothing anyone could tell me that would hinder my stance because it was given to me by the Author of Life.

We are seated with Christ in heavenly places (Ephesians 2:6). As adopted children of God, this is our greater reality. Today, there is a voice that says, "Come up here!" This voice calls us to sit with Christ and to see things—not for what they appear to be—but what they are. Who and what are we letting feed us our perspectives? The news? Tabloids? Horoscopes? Secular (and unfortunately some Christian) sources have, for too long, conditioned us to embrace a reality that breeds fear, hopelessness, and criticism. God wants to fill us with the substance of faith, hope, and love.

What if a generation campaigned for hope in every hopeless situation? With Christ, this is more than possible—it is imperative. If we want to see an awakening in our lifetime, we need to believe God sees potential for life and love in the hardest and darkest places.

I believe that we are supposed to live in hope as we approach seemingly impossible situations. It's easy to become overwhelmed when we are told to ask for the nations as our inheritance. Hopelessness is a poisonous enemy of faith and zeal and shouldn't be given any room in our walks with God.

My heart is for world evangelism. In this chapter, I want to invite you to journey into our Father's heart for every nation and every soul. While you read, let faith arise for a global awakening. Let us become a people who carry the nations in our own hearts until His return.

Stand Before You Go

It's easy to be zealous for a moment, but what does a sustainable zeal for the nations look like? In 2002, God shared His heart with me for Korea. I remember going to the de-militarized zone (DMZ) from the south to the border of the northern line at the 38th parallel. I saw the satellite picture of the Korean peninsula at night. The North, mostly dark with a few lights, looked like a distant constellation, while the southern lights decorated the nation like a Christmas tree. It was such a stark contrast; I knew exactly where the peninsula was split. I remember the Father saying to me, "You'll go into this nation with My light." Little did I know, it would be almost eight years before I would step foot on the land.

The decade that followed was filled with failed attempts of entering the nation, the ebbs and flows of faith-filled intercession, and the developing of patience. But in the midst of all this, God was teaching me that while we are called to "go" into all the earth, we're also called to "stand" in the gap. Ezekiel 22:30, says,

> "And I sought for a man among them who should build up the wall and stand in the breach before me for the land, that I should not destroy it, but I found none" (ESV).

I was deeply impacted when I read this verse recently. God doesn't say, "I only found a few people who would cry out to Me for the land, so I destroyed it." He says, "I found *none*." This verse is beautiful because it invites us to be "the one." Imagine what would happen if we brought a nation before the Lord and committed to praying for the people group of that land. In fact, that's what I want to propose to you. Would you ask the Father to assign you a nation to stand in the gap for? Maybe it's a nation that, for years, you've heard the Spirit call you to. Perhaps it's simply a place that you've always been curious about.

What if you tattooed your heart with that nation and, from here on out, carried it in the place of prayer? Who knows what would be released as you pray to the God who hears you in the secret place? I can imagine the people of that nation, in the great procession before the throne one day, coming to thank you for partnering with the Father to see them come to their heavenly home! It's time for a generation to rise up with faith to take nations! I believe that when you eventually stand before God's judgment seat, you won't hear Him repeat the sobering words that He spoke to Ezekiel—that He searched everywhere, and found none to stand in the gap.

We must go beyond simply praying for that nation. Informed intercessors are like a special force team in the spiritual realm. To pray for a nation without God's heart is like shooting at a target while wearing a blindfold. We may hit the target, but how much more effective could we be if we declared our Father's specific desires for the nations? It doesn't always seem glorious in the moment, but the ability to partner with God's heart in prayer is one of the most overlooked weapons in our spiritual war chest.

We are filled with His zeal, love, and strategies for the nations from a place of intimacy and intercession. Zeal, accompanied by wisdom, wins battles. In hindsight, I realize that if I had jumped into my calling before my time, I would have missed a lot of God's strategy for the nations. If we can maintain a zeal for a people or an issue in the place of prayer, I believe it is an indication that we're ready to be among the sent ones. It is in the furnace of intimacy that a sustainable and pure passion is forged. This passion will enable us to break down the enemy's fortified cities.

My years of study and intercession for the nation of Korea was not merely a waiting period where patience was developed, it was releasing heaven's rain on parched souls all over the peninsula. I'm convinced that dreams and visions of Jesus were released to the citizens of the North. We must pray faith-filled, hope-charged prayers as we wait for His timing to be released to go.

Since my original call to this nation almost a decade ago, I've been able to visit four times in the last two years. You may not have to wait decades before He releases you to physically *go* to be His hands and feet, but let the activation of the Spirit come out of abiding in His heart. After all, Jesus had thirty years before He was released into the most powerful ministry of all.

Our Objective: God's Honor

God is serious about His glory being displayed in the nations, and as His priests on earth, our aim is to see Him glorified. God invites us to co-create with Him, yet our desires for global revival can tend to be polluted with our own motives. What comes to mind when I think of King Saul are stories of how he didn't fear God and responded wrongly to the Lord. While his life can teach us much about poor leadership, in some ways, I feel I may have some similarities.

Saul was zealous for the nation of Israel. Many people would say that we need a leader like Saul who is passionate about the country's well being. While that is true, 2 Samuel 21 tells the story of the "bloodguilt on Saul and on his house, because he put the Gibeonites to death" (ESV). It was because of Saul's sin—when he slaughtered the Gibeonites—that a famine plagued Israel. It turns out that Saul's blind zeal for the nation actually brought about a curse. David, a man after God's own heart, discovered the curse through divine revelation. We don't see any other reference to this event, but my guess is that Saul was probably trying to do God a favor and assumed the command was still to rid the land of the remnant of the Canaanites—in order that Israel might prosper. However, in his zeal and loyalty for a nation, he broke a covenant that had been made four hundred years before between Joshua and the Gibeonites, who were in the land when Israel took possession of it. While the Gibeonites deceived Joshua into making the covenant, it was, nevertheless, a covenant (Joshua 9:3–27).

Covenant keeping was, and continues to be, no small matter to God (Joshua 9:20). Just because God says to take back land for His kingdom, doesn't mean we cease to ask Him how He wants to do it. Do we stop to ask what the history of the land is before we claim and conquer? Heaven is filled with those who have given their lives for revival in the nations; they are a great cloud of witnesses, leaning over the balconies of heaven, wondering how we'll respond. God's desire is to walk in relationship with His creation. Unfortunately, we often prioritize His plans over His presence.

Romans 10:1–4 describes how we can be zealous for God yet be without knowledge. The difference was that while Saul was indeed zealous for the nation of Israel, he wasn't in line with God's wisdom. David, on the other hand, carried a heart for his nation and was also aligned with God's zeal for His honor in the land. David's loyalty was, first and foremost, to God.

As a missionary, I dream about what the nations of the earth could look like after a great spiritual awakening. I love thinking about what will happen when the Dalai Lama (the spiritual leader of the Tibetan Buddhists) comes into a personal relationship with Christ or how the Tibetan monks will someday worship our Lord. However, it's God who holds the keys to the reformation of nations. My zeal and passion for Tibet to be free can never be my primary passion. My primary passion must be obedience to the word of the Lord that comes out of the place of intimacy and informed intercession.

God has blueprints for His glory in the nations; let's ask Him for them. God, what is Your original design for The Netherlands? What will Ireland look like in the midst of revival? What are the sounds that will come from Oman when God's Spirit is poured out on the Omani people?

I'm so thankful for my nation and the blood that was shed purchasing my freedom. However, I feel the most gratitude when I consider that God has granted us citizenship in a heavenly kingdom that will endure forever. All humanity has been sojourners since the Garden of Eden. Yet now, in Christ, we have access back to our original home. I want to fight for the honor of the eternal King and city that will endure when all is made new.

God, in His infinite wisdom, appointed the time and place you would be born. It doesn't matter if you are Canadian, Israeli, or African; He had a purpose in it. We are called to be grateful stewards and citizens of our respective nations. But let us never become loyalists of an earthly inheritance; let's first seek to be patriots for the kingdom of God.

Blessed to Bless Nations

God longs for the world to share in His beauty, fellowship, and blessing. In Genesis, right after God disperses the people at the Tower of Babel, He calls Abram.

In Genesis 12, God tells Abram, "I will make of you a great nation, and I will bless you and make your name great, so that you will be a blessing... and in you **all the families of the earth** shall be blessed" (ESV).

This is good news! God wants to bless us! Why? So that we can bless "all the families of the earth." We're a continuation of this original blessing to Abram. While I believe we're seeing a shift in this, there's still a poverty mentality that creeps into the hearts and minds of believers and prevents us from receiving blessing. If we are unable to receive blessing, how do we expect to *be* a blessing? Sons and daughters of God, through Christ, have access to the throne room and every blessing in the heavenly realms (Ephesians 1:3). Dying to ourselves doesn't mean that we don't receive the crown He places on our heads. It means we have to remember to cast those crowns back down at His feet. God's desire is to bless, and while blessings have a beginning, they're not meant to have an end. The character of God is made clear here—He is in love with all the families of the earth. The initial blessing was bestowed so that the nations would be blessed. Blessing should have momentum. When God pours out favor, it should accompany movement—a sense of "paying it forward."

About six years ago, I had been asking God if I was to help start the movement I'm a part of now called "Awaken." I remember seeing the word "Awaken" superimposed over the horizon at the beach one day. I also remember God clearly guiding me to Luke 12:48. This verse says, "To whom much was given, of him much will be required, and from him to whom they entrusted much, they will demand the more" (ESV). It was evident that I was to help pioneer Awaken, but also that our community would be responsible with "the more." Most of my friends and I were born into privileged families. In fact, I believe the majority of America is truly blessed, but God's goodness and mercy towards us was always meant to be a river of blessing flowing to those in need.

My friends and I joke about FWPs: First World Problems. Sometimes we'll send pictures to each other. One caption, over a picture of a woman with a single tear running down her face, says, "One pillow is too low…two pillows is too high." Another video shows a shivering girl wrapped in a blanket saying "I'm so cold... somebody set the air conditioner to seventy-two degrees; I need it at seventy-three." It's humorous, but all too true. What do we do if we can't find Wi-Fi? How do we respond when our fast food takes more than five minutes to arrive? Let's look beyond our current situations and adopt a nation and its people to channel blessing towards. It's not just the visionary leaders who are called to global perspective. *You* are a world changer. Let's contend for the voiceless in the place of intercession, awareness, and acts of justice. I think this generation is actually very passionate—our passion is simply misdirected!

When I started my missionary journey twelve years ago, I only received support money from others, thinking there was no way that I could give any away. I was barely making my own monthly payments. Then, I felt the Father challenge me saying, "You can't out-give me." I took Him up on that and began to tithe on what was given to me. What I noticed was that I was never lacking. I actually began to support two or three other missionaries in other nations. I've always had enough!

Whether it's finances, spiritual gifts, education, or favor, God's blessing in our lives give us ammunition to be an agent of change to silence injustice. But when a blessing becomes a right, we become stagnant. I believe we're going to see people move from the place of gratitude into the greatest exploits of justice we've ever seen. Father, bless and raise up a nameless, faceless generation to turn a world upside down for You!

Even now, I believe the Holy Spirit can speak to you about how you can see "justice roll down like waters, and righteousness like an ever-flowing stream" (Amos 5:24, ESV). *Ever-flowing!* Let's become rivers of blessing, not stagnant swamps. The nations are waiting!

Get Caught Up in the Story

These two passages—one from the beginning and one from the end—capture God's dream: every tribe, people, and language standing before the throne.

> I will multiply your offspring as the stars of heaven and will give to your offspring all these lands. And in your offspring **all the nations of the earth** shall be blessed. —Genesis 26:4, ESV

> After this I looked, and behold, a great multitude that no one could number, from **every nation, from all tribes and peoples and languages**, standing before the throne and before the Lamb, clothed in white robes, with palm branches in their hands, and crying out with a loud voice, "Salvation belongs to our God who sits on the throne, and to the Lamb!"
> —Revelation 7:9–10, ESV

The beginning and end are written, what lies in between is our inheritance.

> "Ask of me, and I will make **the nations** your heritage, and **the ends of the earth** your possession"
> —Psalm 2:8, ESV

Graciously, He is saying, "Come help me write the story of the nations." This invitation is for everyone; regardless of your location, social status, or gift mix. While you may never actually go to a foreign land, you are heirs in the promise of Psalm 2:8.

Jesus came to clear out the moneychangers in the temple
(Matthew 21:12) because God always intended His temple to be
a house of prayer for *all nations*. Zeal for God's house consumed
Jesus. Now, *we* have become the temples of the Holy Spirit. Have
we allowed our temples to become something other than houses
of prayer? Our temples are to be places of communion with God,
where God's Spirit abides and people encounter Him through our
witness. Have we slowly, but surely, let lesser acts be what we're
known for? How zealous are we in desiring that the ends of the
earth be filled with the glory of God?

It's time to let the same zeal that drove Jesus to violently over-
throwing the pollution of worldly business drive us to joyful repentance of small-minded, selfish pursuits. This is not an attempt
to guilt anyone to religious activity, but to spur you on to becoming a heavenly patriot who contends for God's glory to cover the
earth like the waters cover the seas. We're called to be ministers of
reconciliation: people through whom God can make an appeal.
Are we, personally, and as communities, carrying a passion and
pursuit of God's glory and honor in the nations along with faith
for a global harvest?

One thing is clear: we won't see Jesus return until the Gospel
has reached the whole world. Matthew 24:14 (ESV) says,

> "And this gospel of the kingdom will be proclaimed
> throughout the whole world as a testimony to all
> nations, and then the end will come."

Our longing to see Christ return cannot be separated from
our desire to see His kingdom come to earth here and now. Christ
called all of us to live in and from the place of abiding in Him, and
from here, to "Go into all the world" (Matthew 28:19).

Now, more than ever, the harvest is ready! We've heard it for years. In fact, Jesus said that the harvest was ready two thousand years ago. How much more ready is it now, thousands of years after Jesus said these words? In my twelve years of being a missionary, I have never seen the fields so ripe. Even as I write this, I'm celebrating the fact that last night I had the privilege of leading a Korean family to salvation in Jesus!

Ralph Winter has said that the Bible is not the basis of missions; missions is the basis of the Bible. Today I want to help further set you into motion in regard to some of the planet's hardest and darkest. Do we have the constant *yes* fixed in our hearts to go anywhere and to anyone that the Father would ask us? Righteous zeal for the nations comes from the place of intimacy, and influence in the nations comes from the place of intercession, but we also have to be ready to be the answer to our own prayers. Are we willing to be the laborers sent into the fields that we're asking God for?

Partner with God's Zeal for the Nations

Someday, an expression of every nation, tribe, and tongue will stand before the throne. Jesus' commission was to "Go and make disciples of all nations." Right now, there are over seven thousand unreached people groups: people who have never encountered the saving power and love of Christ.

I want to offer a few practical steps about how you can partner with God's zeal for the nations:

- Ask God for His heart for the nations; ask Him for a broadening of our "world" view.
- Commit to praying for at least *one* nation of the earth (there is a list of unreached people groups info at

www.joshuaproject.net), and be willing to go there if
He calls.

- After asking for God's hope-filled perspective on that
nation, follow what's happening in the news about
that nation. Let faith arise and continue to pray!

- Consider researching missions in an area and sowing
financially into missions in that nation.

My friend, Lindy, penned the song "Every Nation, Every
Soul." In closing I want you to read the following lyrics and let
them paint a picture in your mind.

> All the nations they will come,
> Holding broken chains above their heads.
> Singing, "We have overcome,
> by the blood of the Lamb."
> Jesus, You, You're worth it all
> Every Nation, Every Soul
> All the people will sing your praises,
> All the people will sing your praises,
> All the people will sing your praises,
> "Glory to the Lamb of God!"[3]

The Lamb is worthy to receive the reward of His suffering. He
really is worthy of every nation and every soul. There is so much
hope for every people group of the earth. From across the street
to across the sea, the time for the nations to know their Creator
is now.

About the Author

Andrew and his wife, Terry, are missionaries with Youth With
A Mission. He and a group of committed friends lead a mission-

al-community planting team and multiple discipleship training schools called "Awaken." He has a heart for the nations, longs to see the greatest spiritual awakening happen within America unto the nations, and specifically to see the Koreans revived and reconciled in their relationship with the Father. Find out more about Awaken at www.awakendts.com, and follow Andrew on Twitter @andrewmyork, or contact him at www.andrewmyork.com.

Chapter 9

The Lost Art of Being Diligent

Eric Johnson

I was fifteen years old when Reebok came out with a shoe called the Reebok Pump. Every kid I knew begged their parents to purchase this shoe. The Reebok Pump was a thing of innovation and beauty. The pair that I, myself, drooled over was a black high-top basketball shoe. The design was very eye-catching. My favorite part was the little orange basketball that was on the upper part of the tongue of the shoe. You would pump this little basketball to fill up the built-in airbags in the bottom of the shoe, thus customizing the level of support you wanted for your foot. It was absolutely the coolest shoe in the world.

The Bible teaches about being persistent. Well, I was persistent in my desire to grace my feet with a pair of those amazing shoes. The day came when I went to the store and got my very own pair. Even the shoebox was incredible. If I remember correctly, I heard angels singing when I first opened the box and put the shoes on. It was heaven on earth—at least for me.

I still remember the first day I wore them to school. I had a little strut to go along with the pride in my heart—I was the only kid in school with those shoes. Everyone complimented my shoes. I lost track of the number of times I had to say "thank you" that day.

One day after wrestling practice, I went to my school locker to grab my books and the shoes before I went home. I had put them in there while I was at practice. As I walked up to the locker I saw that it had already been opened. I soon realized that my locker had been broken into and vandalized. In an instant I felt anger and despair. Someone had stolen my prize!

In no time, my friends and I were on the search for my shoes. My angry heart was on a mission to find the thief and see to it that justice was served. I had only owned them for about a week. The next day in school we looked for them all over the place. A few days after they were stolen from my locker, one of the coaches came up and said, "I think I know who took them." It turned out that a student had not only stolen them but had also taken a pen and drawn all over them and cut them up a little bit with a knife— probably to make it look like they were worn and used. At the end of the day, it was obvious that he had stolen them. I was excited that he got caught and the principal was handling the situation.

I remember getting home after school and telling my dad about the kid who stole them, how he had got caught, and how I was *really* happy he had been found out. My dad's response was, "I wonder if he needed a pair of shoes." It turned out that this kid was from an area in town that was really run down, and he lived in poverty. His family didn't have any money to be able to buy him new shoes. My dad's response shocked me at first. I went from feeling justice and wanting revenge to experiencing a heart of compassion. I hadn't guarded my heart; I had allowed it to feel the need for revenge. I started to learn that day that one of the great responsibilities we have as believers is to guard our hearts.

Diligent to Guard Your Heart

I have been a believer for most of my life. I don't remember a part of my life when I wasn't serving God. Through all the years of growing up as a pastor's kid, starting a family of my own, and being in a place of leadership in the church, I can stand here and say that I am more in love with and fascinated by God than I have ever been. There is no other way to spend my life but to serve the King of Kings.

My parents raised my siblings and me with the perspective that our attitude is what we should pay attention to and not just our behavior. Once our attitude was right, then the right behavior would follow. I remember being disciplined; usually Mom or Dad would discipline me for a wrong attitude not because of wrong actions. It taught me something that I now carry over into raising my own children: it's about the heart and not the actions.

When we decide to live a life for the King, the sure fire way to do it well and with passion and love is to do it from the heart. Proverbs 4:23 says, "Keep your heart with all diligence, for out of it flow the issues of life" (NKJV). When you and I begin to diligently guard, protect, and steward our hearts, our actions will fall in line without much effort. Unfortunately, many of us spend a lot of energy on *doing* the right thing, instead of making it a priority to steward our hearts.

On that day when my shoes were found, I vividly remember looking at the thief with a heart of anger, yet in the next moment, I could see his reality of not having anything. I realized maybe he did need a pair of shoes. I somehow understood his situation, and I saw him through the eyes of compassion.

I'm often asked, "How do you stay hungry and passionate for God? How do you have and keep zeal for God?" My answer is, "I guard and steward my heart." This choice, and the resulting action, make it really hard for anyone or anything to offend or derail me from the course on which I have set my life. Oftentimes when we become offended, or thrown off guard, our zeal for the Lord and the kingdom falters. When you guard and steward your heart, you begin to gain a resolve that isn't limited to an emotion. If we reduce zeal and passion to an excited emotion, we will experience a shortfall of seeing a lifestyle of revival.

In my life and ministry, I am exposed to people from all walks of life. It's common to meet people that are in a tough spot in their walk with God. I've seen that many people who are struggling in their walk with God are stuck in a false belief. This belief tells them that in order to be passionate for God, they must be really excited all the time. They try hard to be passionate and to do the right things for God. They base their passion and zeal for God on how excited they are about Him. The issue with this is when they aren't experiencing an excited emotion and they can't conjure it up, they usually feel like they are failing or even neglecting God.

Diligence apart from love is performance and striving. Diligence with love and grace at its core creates an unshakeable foundation for a lifestyle of zeal and passion. I don't measure my passion and zeal on how excited I feel; I measure it by the health of my heart. When I go through my life, I don't look at all the high moments or the low moments. I look at how I stewarded my heart in each of those moments. When we choose to do this, we begin to see a lifestyle of zeal and passion for revival emerge and burn in our hearts for a lifetime.

Diligent to Stay Tapped into the Source

One of the keys to living with diligence founded on love and grace is to tap into the Source. When you begin to experience the grace of God, not just in theory, but also in your spirit and emotions, something shifts. The seasons of life may shift and change, you may experience highs and lows, but one thing remains, and that is the grace of God. Many believers are relying on the external things to happen in order for the internal reality to be thriving. That's backwards. When you are connected to the Source, which is God Himself, the only One that is unshakable, you begin to thrive in all the seasons of life. You could be in the worst season or surrounded by horrible circumstances yet be thriving in your heart. Not out of ignorance of your reality, but because you are tapped into something that doesn't live on the circumstances of external realities.

Look at the life of Jesus. One of the obvious things about Him was that no matter what He was confronted with, be it sickness, food shortage, natural disaster, money issues, or death, He brought the solution. He was able to do this because He was in direct connection with the Father. Many times in the Gospels, we see Jesus saying, "I only do what I see the Father doing." This is another way of saying, "I am always in connection with Him, and I am aware of what He is doing at all times." Because of this, He was able to do what He did in His life. We have the same access to the Father. When we recognize that, we will see pure diligence and zeal come forth.

So what does tapping into the Source look like? How do we come to a place to be able to say, "I only do what I see the Father doing"? Let me use the illustration of my marriage. Some people ask me about my wife: what she likes to do or what she would do in certain situations. I am only able to answer these questions because I have spent time with her, listened to her, and watched what she does in certain situations. It's quite simple, but this is where it starts. Some of us have been so driven by our personal goals in life that we don't know what *God* wants or what He's thinking. As believers, we must create space for time with God: find our secret place with Him. For some, it's outside while jogging, and for others, it's being in a prayer chapel. Whatever and wherever it is, make it a top priority.

True diligence comes from a deep conviction of knowing what is possible and what is true. Then, when we plug into the Source, God Himself, we will experience a deep conviction and awareness of the true reality of who we are in Christ. Living from this place causes men and women of God to do things that are humanly impossible.

David, the boy who defeated Goliath, was one of those people. When Goliath started mocking David's God, David was stirred up with a zeal that altered the course of Israel's history. Aimee Semple McPherson had the impossible vision to build an immense house for God in the middle of the Great Depression. Her vision exists in solid form today as the Angelus Temple. Martin Luther King, Jr. saw something in his heart: a nation where all races of people could gather together and celebrate life. Evan Roberts was touched by God to bring revival to Wales—a revival that has since been referred to as one of the greatest revivals ever known to man. All these individuals were known for their diligence and zeal, but it was because they tapped into the Source that allowed them to live out these incredible lives.

Things change when you go through life connected to God. Your thoughts, emotions, and your spirit begin to be shaped in such a way that you no longer question what is possible, but instead you seek to make the impossible become reality. Your identity begins to be shaped according to the way the kingdom of God works. The New Covenant believer is different from the Old Covenant believer. In the Old Covenant, what you touched would affect you. For example, you were instructed to not touch a leper because it would make you unclean. In the New Covenant, you touch the leper, and they become clean. When you no longer live under the law and are living under grace, you bring light, life, hope, and healing into any situation.

Being diligent in your walk with God and in a lifestyle of revival must be rooted in the heart of God. This is the kind of diligence that compels you to take on the giants of your day. If you cultivate this kind of diligence, it has the potential to ignite the generations of people that you will never see.. They will look back on your life, and it will move them to a place of pure diligence and zeal. This is what we are looking for in this generation today: to walk in such a measure of diligence and zeal that they shape the course of history. So when the end of your life comes, you can stand there and say, "I was faithful with what the Lord gave me, and I didn't falter or waiver from the course that was set before me."

Diligent to Burn for a Lifetime

Some years back, my dad mentioned something to our students in Bethel School of Supernatural Ministry (BSSM). He said, "Come find me in twenty years and tell me you're still burning for revival." This was a challenge to burn for revival for a lifetime not just a moment.

My wife, Candace, and I travel to Norway every year or two. We speak at a conference that dedicates one afternoon to a gathering of former BSSM students. The name of the gathering is *Still Burning*. During this connection time, we simply hang out and see how everyone is doing and what God is doing in their lives. Usually, we have over forty former students from the different Scandinavian countries that fly in for the time together.

On our most recent trip, we had the highest attendance to date, since there are more and more Scandinavian students coming to our school and then returning home. We noticed something interesting: the students that had been back in their country for three years or more were doing well and beginning to really thrive. But most of the students that had been back home for less than three years were having a really hard time being home, and some were trying to find ways to leave. Most of the stories sound something like this: "It is really hard coming back to the culture and being successful with all the things we learned in BSSM."

Candace and I began to ask the students that had been home for three years or more to tell the other students what they had personally done that had helped them navigate the first few years of being home. All of them replied with answers like this: get close to God, hear His heart and truth, and stay connected to others that are burning. They tapped into the Source and protected that connection, which helped them not waiver or falter when everything in them cried out to give up. Now, they are able to say they are thriving.

To truly live in zeal for the Lord, we must fully live from a place of pure devotion and diligence in our relationship with

Him. When we get a resolve in our heart for the King—when we are diligent in our relationship with Him—we experience a passion and zeal that is not based on whether our days are good or bad. but is based on something much deeper. It is based on something that is immovable and unshakeable: the heart of God. So let's keep this in mind and be diligent with our lives.

About Eric Johnson

Eric serves on the senior leadership for Bethel Church in Redding, California. He and his wife, Candace, are the senior leaders over the local church—Bethel Redding. He is a sixth-generation minister and has authored *Momentum: What God Starts Never Ends*. Eric and Candace have a passion to see transformation take place in the lives of people, cities, and nations. They are the proud parents of two beautiful daughters. Connect with Eric at www. BethelRedding.com and on Twitter @ericbj.

Chapter 10

Obtaining Promises

Aaron Walsh

A s I looked around the San Francisco Airport, I could barely comprehend what was happening. I was about to board a plane to Redding, California. This was the fulfillment of a prophetic dream I had had one-year prior. In this dream I was sharing at a large meeting about a nation in Africa where everyone who received prayer got healed. While I was sharing, Bill Johnson stood up and announced, "God is going to do this in New Zealand and I will help you."

I woke up and knew immediately that God had just given us a significant promise. I also knew that I needed to get to Redding to visit Bethel Church where Bill was leading. The community at Bethel had experienced breakthrough in the realms of miracles and healing and I was hungry for that to occur in New Zealand.

Sitting in the airport that evening, waiting to board the plane to Redding, I received a phone call from my wife, Kristi, who was back home in New Zealand. She told me that she had been admitted to the hospital with severe discomfort in her lower back and hip region. The doctors were unsure what was causing her pain, but they thought that perhaps there was something going on that was far more intense than a simple back injury. I was immediately dismissive that it was anything serious. After all, I was going to inherit a promise. God had led us and provided a way for me to get Redding. It was just as the dream proclaimed: I was going to get anointed and equipped to see miracles flow through New Zealand. It was time for the promise to be obtained.

Landing in Redding after the short flight from San Francisco I saw that I had received a text message during the flight. I didn't want to look at my phone. My wife knew I was flying and a text message meant there was something I needed to know. The message was simple: "Call me ASAP." I knew something must be very wrong. My heart sank and I thought, "I must be dreaming, this can't be real, this can't be happening." My wife was only twenty-nine years old. How is this going to impact our two young children? As I dialed the number I was greeted with the brave but trembling voice of my beautiful wife. "Honey, I have some bad news. The doctors aren't one hundred percent sure, but it is almost certain that I have multiple sclerosis."

Over the next few days God spoke very clearly. He was going to come with power and heal my wife's fragile body. The morning after my arrival in Redding, I heard of a notable miracle that recently occurred in the healing rooms at Bethel. A woman in a wheelchair began to walk for the first time in ten years. She was healed from multiple sclerosis. In that moment of pain and confusion God had released a simple miracle and declared His intention towards us.

Returning home to New Zealand after my visit to Bethel, the medical tests confirmed what the doctors already knew: multiple sclerosis. These two words from our neurologist changed our lives in one moment. Yes, there was a sense a pain and loss, but a greater prospect gripped our hearts. The pursuit of a promise had begun. We were setting ourselves to run into the hands and heart of God. But we were seeking more than a simple a miracle that would heal my wife's body, we were contending for a promised move of power that would destroy sickness and disease in our nation.

Everyone has a promise from God. Scripture tells us in 2 Corinthians 1:20 that all the promises of God are "Yes and Amen." God intends to answer and fulfill every promise He has made. I believe this is the lens through which we are to view all God's promises. He is the God that fulfills promises and He is the God that answers prayer. He is good. He leads our lives perfectly. This must be our starting point as we relate to God in our pursuit of promises. His promises are underpinned by this certainty: He has power to achieve all He desires and He has no enemies that are powerful enough to prevent His will. Without this raw faith in the ability of God we will have a very fragile foundation to build our pursuit upon.

Delays Are Common

We often experience a time of waiting while we anticipate our promises. It seems that delays play an incredibly important and integral role in the securing of our promises. It is difficult, and often confusing, to simply *wait* when we see someone who is in need of a miracle. This is especially true in the crucible of physical infirmity when there is such an acute awareness of the great need for God to sustain and ultimately heal.

From the narrative of Scripture a very clear pattern emerges. The time between the release of a promise and the fulfillment of a promise is often lengthy. In Luke 18 Jesus Himself addresses this reality in the parable of the persistent widow. The parable has a very clear goal: to encourage people to remain tenacious in their pursuit of God and not lose heart. At the end of the parable Jesus says, "And shall God not avenge His own elect who cry out day and night to Him, though He bears long with them" (Luke 18:7, NKJV). Jesus wants us to understand that often it is necessary to remain faithful and zealous for a longer than we anticipate. A moment of deliverance can come after a long time of waiting.

If this is true, how then do we live in the daily tension of pursing and waiting on promises? What do we do in the delay between the release of the promise and the inheriting of the promise? What do I do when I see my wife struggling to walk on a daily basis? How do we remain zealous in the midst of challenging circumstances without retreating into unbelief? How do we navigate through the mundane without becoming apathetic? How do I keep my heart unoffended toward God in the midst of waiting for my wife to be healed? If we don't grasp God's ways in the obtaining of promises we leave ourselves open to discouragement and accusation in the delay.

Many believers today have a fatalistic mindset when it comes to their God-given promises. The years of waiting have eroded the trust and confidence they once had in God. The promise is adjusted and the pursuit slowly deceases. However, if, while we wait, we are able to remain in zeal then we can contend wholeheartedly with ruthless trust in the goodness of God. We are able to navigate through pain and perplexity without offense and we retain a stubborn refusal to let go of the fullness that God has ordained for us.

Faith and Patience Required

I believe the writer of the book of Hebrews understood this tension well. In Hebrews 6:12 we see the beautiful explanation of this reality. We are exhorted not to be sluggish but to intimidate those who have gone before us and inherited their promises through faith and patience. Most of us have read numerous books or heard sermons on the subject of faith and breakthrough, but I would imagine very few of us would be familiar with the role patience plays in the inheriting of promises.

The book of Hebrews grants us insight into the importance of faith. Hebrews 11:6 says that without faith it is impossible to please God. That statement alone reveals the importance of faith in the kingdom. If we don't have faith we are not pleasing God.

Faith Pleases God

My favorite definition of faith comes from the story of Abraham. Paul points to this story as he writes to the church at Rome about faith. The heart posture of Abraham is described this way: "He grew strong in his faith as he gave glory to God, fully convinced that what God had promised He was also able to perform" (Romans 4:20–21, NKJV). Talk about an impossible promise. Imagine being one hundred years old and receiving a promise that God was about to enlarge your natural family. Imagine looking at your wife, who was ninety-five years old and barren, and being told that she was going to be the vessel in which that promise would be fulfilled.

For Abraham, faith was the ability to not be governed by the impossibility of the situation. God's prophetic promise was so radical to Abraham that there was absolutely nothing Abraham could do in the natural to see the promise come to pass. Radical promises require radical faith. For me, watching my wife's body being overtaken by a debilitating disease has redefined faith. It's more than optimism or whimsical hope. My faith has become violent and vulnerable. It's a war against an accuser who subtly draws us into resignation that things will never change. Faith is the ability to not allow the temporal and subjective realities of sickness, disease, and heartache to become permanent and concrete.

Most of us can understand and embrace a promise that we could bring about in our own strength. For each of us, there comes a day when God invites us into a promise that far transcends our natural abilities and resources. He calls us into a ruthless vulnerability and trust. For some people that promise comes through the deepest pain and need. It is one thing when God gives you a promise of how He wants to use you and how you will have magnificent breakthrough. I love those promises. However, it's a whole different reality when your life depends on a promise coming to pass.

Psychologists explain that acceptance is the final stage of grief. Apparently acceptance allows us to cope and move on. As believers in the midst of waiting, and even in the face of death, we are not called to cope. We are called to endure. Coping has no hope, it tells us that this is the new reality and we need to adjust and not expect things to be how they once were. Enduring faces pain from a completely different place. It lives with the promise that what we are facing is temporal: simply one word from heaven can change everything. It doesn't deny pain or confusion, but it refuses to allow it to be the dominant and defining reality. It lives with the knowledge that God will restore everything that was lost. It hopes and believes with joy and zeal and it waits with confidence.

Before Kristi was diagnosed with MS, she loved to run. Where we live in New Zealand there is a beautiful outcrop of seaboard called Mount Maunganui. At the end of the peninsula is a hill that climbs four hundred meters above the ocean. The summit offers the most incredible vista: views out over the Pacific Ocean and along the spectacular New Zealand coastline. A few times a week, she would run up the stairs to the very top. It offers an incredibly tough workout and a real sense of accomplishment.

As we wait on her healing, we are contending for an impossibility. We are looking for a day where her body inherits a promise. A promise that Jesus will rule and reign over disease and make a mockery of multiple sclerosis. Faith doesn't look at a body that can barely walk a few hundred yards and declare that to be reality forever. It looks at a fully restored, fully healthy body sprinting over the crest of Mount Maunganui, rejoicing and celebrating the impossible. Faith looks for the day where she can play and run with our kids, and our children having an amazing testimony of witnessing the miracle of God healing their mum.

Patience Produces Humility in Victory

What then is the role of patience? If you are like me, you find patience an incredibly difficult trait to embrace. I am the type of person who hates waiting for anything. I want it done in my time frame. One thing the narrative of scripture reveals is God rarely does things when we think He should. Scripture also reveals that man's attempts to produce God's promises always end in failure. It is natural in our zeal to try and obtain our promise outside of God's timing. It doesn't work. The failure is necessary.

During these times, God is doing something profound in us. He is tenderly eliminating our desire to take credit for our own breakthrough. Paul understood this principle. In writing to the church at Corinth, he confronts an arrogance that has caused division. The saints were defining themselves by the person they were following. Some were saying they were disciples of Paul and some were saying they were disciples of Apollos. As a result envy, strife, and division had emerged. Paul writes to them and explains the process: "Who then is Paul, and who then is Apollos, but ministers through who you believed, as the Lord gave to each one? I planted, Apollos watered, but the Lord gave increase. So then neither he who plants is anything, nor he who waters, but God who gives increase" (1 Corinthians 3:5–7, NKJV).

What Paul is saying is stunning. He is comparing the work of Apollos and himself as nothing, compared to the work of the Lord in the people he was leading. He saw the planting and watering as necessary, but it was the work of the Lord that produced increase. Paul almost singlehandedly led and nurtured the early church from nothing into a global force that turned the world upside-down in one generation. However, Paul refused to see himself as the reason for impossible growth and breakthrough.

God won't allow us to see ourselves as the reason for increase; He will not allow us to see ourselves as the key for our breakthrough. He loves us so much that He will not grant us our inheritance if it will injure us. Human zeal tempts us to take a promise, apprehend it immediately, and then tell everyone how we accomplished it. Godly zeal plants and waters faithfully, year after year, knowing that God is working to produce in them a heart that can steward radical victory with radical humility.

One of the more rare and beautiful things on this earth is victory received with humility. The emergence of humility is impossible without failure. Peter was promised leadership in the early church. He thought he could inherit that promise by sheer force. When Peter brandished his sword against the crowd coming to arrest Jesus and cut off the ear of a solider, he was trying to show Jesus that he was capable. However, Jesus was not looking for capable men to lead His church. He was looking for humble men. It wasn't until the dramatic public failure of his own denial of Christ that Peter became qualified to lead the church and enter into his promise. He had to be broken in order to see his true condition and acknowledge his great need.

In our journey, we have also come to understand the crucible of waiting. God is not punishing us; He is preparing us. Often our inheritance or promise is beyond anything we could comprehend. When we say "Yes" to the promise, we also say "Yes" to the process by which God leads us into our promise draped in humility. God wants our lives to be so deeply rooted in Him that we are not moved when breakthrough comes.

Faith and patience are married in the pursuit of promises. If we have faith without patience, we end up living in disappointment and accusation when the promises don't come to pass in our expected time frame. We conclude that God is not faithful and we can't trust His promises. We insulate our hearts against disappointment. The radical trust and vulnerability is gone and we live predictable, boring lives. But if we have patience without faith, we fall into apathy and unbelief. We stop contending and inadvertently embrace our condition as permanent. We adjust our posture and slowly hope dissipates.

Live Courageously While You Wait

When we live in faith and patience, we are able to possess radical zeal. Zeal is deep and consuming. Zeal empowers us to fully pursue the word of the Lord while fully embracing the ways of God. As we wait on promises, we must embrace a life of courageous zeal. We have such a limited understanding of courage. Courage is not jumping out of airplanes or climbing insanely high mountains. It is much more than that. From the perspective of a believer, courage is incredibly important. We see regularly in Scripture the call to be courageous and strong in the Lord. Courage is when we bind ourselves to the Word and ways of God until the promises comes to pass.

The Lord called Joshua to be courageous. His promise was that he would enter into a foreign land known for its fierce reputation. Though frightened, Joshua courageously embraced the promise. He chose to bind himself to God and not be moved by the opposition. In doing so, Joshua ensured the promise would become a reality.

We all face the temptation to retreat from our promises. We all know how easy it is to stop contending for the fullness. Our own family is believing for healing with faith. We are contending and longing for the day of promise—the day where power from another realm will take a broken body and make it well. It is a promise we are to obtain. It is a promise that has been written into the story of our lives. It is a promise that will open a well of healing for many.

Sitting here today, three years after the initial diagnosis, we are yet to see healing, but we are learning to walk in faith and patience. The Lord has upheld us by unimaginable grace and kindness, and He will continue to do so. We live for the day where justice will prevail. We wait in zeal to obtain the promise.

About the Author

The Lord called Aaron Walsh, a native of New Zealand, to Kansas City in 1998 to help pioneer what developed into the International House of Prayer, launching and participating in IHOP-KC's first internship in 1999. He returned to New Zealand in 2006 as the Lord called him and his family to establish the house of the Lord in the ends of the earth. Again pioneering a house of prayer, he now serves as the director of a house of prayer and associate leader of Hope Centre Tauranga. Connect with and follow Aaron on twitter @Aaron_Walsh1.

Chapter 11

Always Pioneering
with Zeal

Roger Joyner

Ilost my father when I was two years old. He was tormented by demons and believed that he could protect me by taking his own life. He committed suicide on the day that my mom went to abort my unborn sibling. The trauma of losing my father marked me with rage, rejection, and sexual confusion. I didn't know who I was, and I tried to "find myself" in many different places. I made many subcultures my home for a season in the search for a place of identity.

In 1998, I gave my heart back to Jesus. I had lived a life of rebellion and anger toward my mom; I blamed her for my dad's suicide. God turned my heart back to my mom, and I forgave her for the abortion and the loss of my dad. I also asked her to forgive me for the pain I had caused her. Later, when I joined Youth With A Mission (YWAM) for a Discipleship Training School (DTS), my heart was healed even more.

During my DTS, Bethel pastor Bill Johnson prophesied over me that God was taking my scars and turning them into His crystals. He said that I would be like Abraham—a father of many nations. I felt His purpose in the midst of pain and His fiery heart for redemption. It was in this moment that I realized that God could redeem my pain and use it for His glory. Although I lost my own father, God had a plan to make me a spiritual father to many.

I began to be filled with a zeal for the purposes of God in my generation. I would spend my time praying for my generation—that they would experience healing and turn their hearts back to their fathers and mothers. I prayed that God would raise up an army of mothers and fathers who would reach out to the broken generation, know their deep personal pain, and love them through it. I was gripped by that flame, and I knew I had to steward it.

It was during this time I met a man who was truly like a father to me: a man named John Knoch. He became deeply aware of my pain and discipled me towards life, healing, and restoration. John pointed my eyes to the plans and dreams of God in my generation and encouraged me that I was destined to see God's purposes come to pass.

I surrendered my past and became a man—finally emerging out from under the crushing pain of fatherlessness. God made me a carrier of the Father's heart. He set my heart on fire with zeal for the fatherless. I wanted desperately for God to touch the lost, for the Spirit of adoption to break in on our generation, and for my peers to know God as Father. Getting to know the greatest

Father ever transformed my wound from not knowing my dad into a wound of love. My greatest pain became my entrance into knowing Him.

This wound of love is a torch I carry with me always—that many sons would be brought to glory, and that we would know Him as Father unlike any other time in history. Around the same time, a gathering took place that would help shape the course of my life.

The Call D.C.

In 1999, an epic summoning was given to America: over half a million young adults and parents gathered to build an altar for an awakening in America. Many, including myself, gave a year to intense fasting and prayer to prepare for the event—The Call D.C. The day itself was one of the holiest, most intense things I have ever experienced as we wept, fasted, and dedicated our lives to the mandate of turning a nation back to God.

Many were launched into a life call of separation to live uncompromised lives. They left that mall in Washington D.C. with a heart set on a pilgrimage of awakening in America. A whole new breed of pioneers was born in that season of time. These were not pioneers who were disconnected from the rich, spiritual history of our nation, but those freshly reconnected to the same zeal that gave birth to America and its many outpourings and renewals. A new generation consecrated their lives as an altar for the fire of revival to once again fall on America. We committed our lives as pioneers to this end. I am seeing this same resurgence once again.

A New Breed of Pioneers

There is a new breed of pioneers rising. They have given their hearts to serving the purposes of God in their generation. They are fueled through encounters with His voice and have set their hearts to be an epic force for revival. They strive to sow where no one has sown, and they live their lives as ones who prepare the way for the greatest outpouring the world has seen.

They have found each other in deep-hearted friendship as fellow pilgrims on a legendary journey. They dream of the salvation of the planet, and their hearts are bonfires of passion for God. They live in the place of encouragement: emboldening others as they offer courage from the reality of their intimacy with God. As pioneers, they carry a steadfast focus and an unwillingness to back down from the fulfillment of God's purposes in their generation. They have the deep knowledge that relationship with God is a journey of hearing and pursuing His heart.

These pioneers know that when God speaks, He opens our ears and stirs a holy zeal. They understand that God plants a seed, waters it, and watches over it as it becomes a tree bearing great fruit. They experience an unquenchable longing for Him and His holiness. This holy zeal begins to take over and direct the course of their entire lives. They know that through encountering God, hearing His heart, and feeling His love, we become one with His desire. These encounters become the very sparks that set them on the journey.

The Spark of a Pioneer

The first time I heard the voice of God was when I was reading about the boy, Samuel in the Bible. As my heart was moved by the story, I heard God say, "Roger, your mom dedicated you to Me like Samuel's mother did, and you also are called to be a preacher." I remember running and asking my mom, "Did you dedicate me to God like Samuel?" She told me she did. That next morning during the church service, I announced that God had called me to be a preacher. This experience clearly showed me that we could hear the voice of God.

The spark of the pioneer happens when we have an encounter with God that draws us into a larger picture. These encounters catch us up in a whirlwind, and we are swept out of the mundane. Through them, we experience God's call to see His purposes fulfilled. We will be led to take risks and do things we never dreamed possible. These sparks can happen in a gathering or in a room alone with God. But it is hunger and attentiveness that sets a stage for it. Once you get that spark, guard it with all you've got!

There is a quote I like from Elizabeth Barrett Browning: "Earth's crammed with heaven, and every common bush afire with God; but only he who sees, takes off his shoes—the rest sit 'round it and pluck blackberries."[4] Being attentive to His voice sets us apart from the normal day-to-day routine. When we turn to see and focus on the "burning bush" of encounter with God, He calls out our names and brings us into a larger storyline of history making.

When God speaks to you, it is a holy thing, and it is a place of sacred worship. We have to steward these encounters or else the birds of the air, the cares of life, or the whispers of the enemy will try to convince us that we are madmen who made it all up. We must treat these encounters as holy moments: we are not a part of the blackberry-pickers.

It's been fourteen years since The Call, D.C. My heart remains convinced that a whole nation can turn to God. I know the God I encountered, and no man, demon, or life circumstance can rob it from my heart.

Zeal to Steward God's Voice

Two things set a pioneer or a forerunner apart from the crowd. The first is "spiritual violence:" a holy zeal to not let any lesser passion rob the appetite for God. The second is the way in which the pioneer treats the Word of the Lord. In a letter to Timothy, Paul exhorts him to take his personal prophecies seriously. "This charge I commit to you, son Timothy, according to the prophecies previously made concerning you, that by them you may wage the good warfare" (1 Timothy 1:18, NKJV). What we do with our prophecies determines the weight of the impact it has on our lives. We must be careful not to let them simply sit on the shelf and become just another good story. If we use them as weapons of warfare, they can create a wineskin and an atmosphere of faith to contain a move of God's Spirit.

Stewarded, these encounters become a deep well of water to drink from. They will constantly refresh and remind us of God's heart and longing for each of us. When we drink it in, it makes us rise once again with confidence, hungry for fresh encounters of intimacy with Him. He causes us to develop deep roots in Him— like strong trees planted by the streams of living water—sheltering others and releasing fruitfulness.

Encountering God's Zeal in His Word

When you are reading the Bible and you see a promise that is unfulfilled, let it provoke you to prayer and action. Let a groan arise inside of you. Jesus rebuked the Pharisees because they studied the Word of God but they didn't come near to God. When a verse grabs your heart, draw near to God. There is a time to be still before God, but don't be afraid to make strong declarations loudly in prayer to God. There is something that happens in your spirit and heart when you shout out His Word in prayer!

> He shall see the labor of His soul, and be satisfied.
> By His knowledge My righteous Servant shall justify
> many. —Isaiah 53:11, NKJV

Has Jesus received the full reward of all of the nations of the earth? Begin to cry out, "God, You said You would see the labor of Your soul and be satisfied. Let my generation see the labor of Your soul. Let my city see the labor of Your soul and be satisfied. Release the outpouring of Your love, God. Jesus, receive Your reward!"

> Who has believed our report? And to whom has the
> arm of the Lord been revealed? —Isaiah 53:1, NKJV

Has the arm of the Lord been revealed to all those in our generation (all those who are living)? Are there injustices that need the arm of God to be displayed? Let this stir your heart and cultivate the desire for the fulfillment of God's Word. Let it make you a flame that refuses to accept passivity. How long will our cities be claimed by the fog of darkness? Begin to let the promises of God make you groan inside, "God reveal Your arm to my generation, shake this nation with Your power, show Yourself and topple drug addiction, topple sexual confusion. Break rejection off a generation! Release a spirit of adoption. God, reveal Your arm and show us Your power like You did before. Let the people walking in darkness see a great light."

Armed with prayers like this, you begin to create an atmosphere of revelation and you become the bright beacons of global outpouring. I want to provoke you to be a pioneer: a hinge of history. As Lou Engle has said, "There are moments in history when a door for massive change opens, and great revolutions, for good or evil, spring up in the vacuum created by these openings.

In these divine moments, key men and women and even entire generations risk everything to become the hinge of history—the pivotal point that determines which way the door will swing."[5]

Cultivate Zeal by Reading History

It's important to read the stories of God's power being released and shaking regions like the book of Acts. Read the stories of injustice being conquered. But don't just read revival history— let history possess you. Let the stories provoke a cry within you, for the God of history is reaching for you, whispering, "Let Me loose again." Your prayers can move angels into position and push apathy off of believers. When we allow the great works of God to motivate us, then prayer meetings will begin to break out for revival. Study the works of the Lord and take great delight in them. Delight yourself in His works and the moves of revival. This has been one of the key ways that I have cultivated a zeal for prayer and revival. Become acquainted with His heart to come in power, for you are written into the storyline.

Hebrews 11:39–40 says, "And all these, having obtained a good testimony through faith, did not receive the promise, God having provided something better for us, that they should not be made perfect apart from us." The author of Hebrews is explaining that the works of our current generation can act as a fulfillment of the dreams of the generations that came before us. You are invited into God's story.

The Daily Bread of the Voice of God

We were created to know the thoughts of God toward us; this is key for young pioneers. In the midst of our burning focus, we must remember that we were created to hear the sound of His voice. Jesus confirms this in John 4:4 when He says, "It is written,

'Man shall not live by bread alone, but by every word that proceeds from the mouth of God.'"

God created us to hear His voice, and we are unable to sustain zeal without consistently hearing His heart and His thoughts. His voice washes us from losing intimacy by the mission. Intimacy *is* the mission. His voice and nearness remind us that He loves to invade our days: plow the field of our hearts so we are soft again.

His Word is God-breathed, exciting, and full of His emotion. Jesus is God's Word made flesh so that we can taste and see the reality of who He is. Many have set out touched by God's voice and filled with ambition, but have ended up jaded and burnt out. It is important that we sustain our zeal by the daily encounter with God.

Psalm 139 is a radical account of God intimately knowing us. Having this view of His attentiveness toward us can cause us to rest in the reality of His goodness and desire to meet with us:

> Your eyes saw my substance, being yet unformed. And in Your book they all were written, the days fashioned for me, when as yet there were none of them. How precious also are Your thoughts to me, O God! How great is the sum of them! If I should count them, they would be more in number than the sand; when I awake, I am still with You. —Psalm 139:16–18, NKJV

I love prophecy and hearing the voice of God. It fills my heart with zeal when I see the reality of God and His attentiveness to the small details of life that may seem trivial. One of the most intimate moments that I had of God breaking into my mundane, day-to-day life was when I was a young, single man of about twenty-one. I was freshly pursuing God, and my heart was on fire for prayer and revival. I spent most of my days and nights crying out to God for an awakening in my generation and my nation. I was renting a small place and working a minimum wage job at McDonald's. A covenant friend and I would pray and do outreach like madmen. That season of blazing in zeal was one of the favorite times in my life.

I needed a shower curtain and rod for my bathroom, but, being a bachelor, I decided I would take showers without one and just mop up afterwards with towels. My mom bought me a curtain and rod, but when I took it into the bathroom to hang it up, I was disappointed because the rod was too short.

Shortly afterwards, my covenant-revivalist friend, Joseph Sielaff, came to spend the weekend with me from the YWAM base. He told me how he was trying to press into God in prayer. He was frustrated because he was trying to hear God and really give himself to intercession. He told me that he'd had a daydream about me getting a shower curtain rod that was too short. He said that in this daydream all he had to do was twist the curtain rod and it would lengthen.

The crazy thing about this was he didn't know I had just gotten a shower curtain rod. I brought it to him, he twisted it, and it worked! I was so excited that God cared for me so much He even gave my friend a vision about my problem while in prayer. Here we were filled with zeal for outpouring and revival, and He was filled with zeal to overwhelm us with how real He is. When we become aware that He is intimately acquainted with all our ways, it creates a rest in our zeal that is not rooted in the strength of our swing but the nearness of God!

Finding Your Covenant Company

One of the most important scriptures that has become a reality to me that I think is especially important for a new breed of pioneers is Psalm 68:6 (NIV): "He sets the lonely in families, he leads out the prisoners with singing, but he makes the rebellious live in a sun-scorched land."

In 2003, I attended The Call School of Ministry in California led by Lou Engle. I was brought under the leadership of a man who modeled a lifetime of zeal for revival and attentiveness to the voice of God. I was swept into a company of young people who had, in a sense, sold it all in consecration for the great purpose of awakening and revival in America. The day I arrived, Lou and his longtime covenant friend were sharing about their history of deep friendship. They were leading the group in taking communion and entering a place of covenant with each other in preparation for walking the trail of tears on a prophetic prayer journey. We covenanted that we would walk with one another in love; if we had an issue with each other, we would go to each other and resolve it rather than harboring offense or talking to others about the offense.

As they were leading the time together, they recounted a dream. In the dream, the greatest revival that the world had ever seen was behind a door. The door had a combination lock and, instead of numbers, there were letters. They dialed in the word *covenant* and the door opened! As they recounted the dream, I wept. I was receiving a key that would lead the rest of my life. I didn't know at the time what I was receiving. I felt the weight of it but couldn't tell anyone at the time why.

I wept as I realized I had been burning in secret and knew God was destroying my loneliness by setting me in a family. I had found my company: the dreamers, those who were given to zeal, who wanted to know how hot they could blaze and how intensely they could give themselves to revival and breakthrough for a nation. The Lord told me you make covenant with those whose dreams and heart you connect with.

This prophetic community became a greenhouse for my zeal. It became a place where I become courageous in my calling—a place in which I became zealous for my friends' destinies as well. They became my comrades-in-arms and my family. Most of us are married now and have our own families, but there is still a love between us that is more real than I have experienced. We've been through many changes and done more prophetic prayer strikes as a community of people than I can remember. But our hearts bearing one another's burdens and carrying each other's dreams has brought massive healing and created a context for zeal to be sustained.

We still can call each other, and in a moment feel like we have never left each other's sides. Probably one of the most key elements in my life to sustaining zeal is this covenant community where we are deeply known and deeply know others. We have changed ministry names, birthed JHOP, Bound4LIFE, The Call, The Cause, and Red Riders. The names and some of the ministries have come and gone, but the heart for each other has remained. This part of the church is so crucial for a generation whose families have often been damaged. I've been healed and seen others radically healed. I've even seen their natural families restored as some of the fruit.

I'll never forget meeting the *Burn* tribe for the first time at a summit. Having been invited in by Sean Feucht, I again wept to see such a company possessed with zeal, joy, and faith for America, their cities, and the nations. It revived my heart to see the zeal and purity.

Such companies will change the earth—bands of people who lock together in heart, who fan each other into flame, who care about the bonfire of God's flame and each other's heart more than their own personal flame. The Burn movement is truly such a tribe. It is my tribe.

Pioneering with Zeal

In conclusion, let's take a few moments to reflect and consider a few questions and recommendations that I believe will help you walk out a pioneering life of zeal with God.

- What initiated your spark of zeal to follow God with intensity?

- How are you doing in creating space for God to encounter you?

- How often do you remind yourself and God of His promises and re-stir your heart to the promises He has spoken to you? Do it more!

- I really encourage you to read the Bible out loud to God. For me, the book of Psalms is filled with stuff that connects my heart to His. Especially Psalm 18 and Hebrews 11 stir me to be a hero of the faith. Try it! There is a place for quiet meditation, but there is also a time to roar. If you are not normally one who prays out loud or loudly, try it. Something about that engagement stokes the fire of zeal! Wesley Campbell's book "Praying the Bible" is a great resource for this.

- Pick up a life story of a revivalist, an abolitionist, or a missionary. This will help fan your heart into a flame. As you read, pay attention to their weaknesses and strengths. God doesn't wait for the strong and mighty—just for those who respond to Him in faith.

- If you are not a part of a community, find a community of those who are like-hearted. If your area doesn't have a community, consider joining a Burn community nearby (www.burn24-7.com) or a Fire and Fragrance school (www.fireandfragrance.com). Training schools are a good entrance place to find community and are invaluable for stewarding your zeal.

Final Prayer

Jesus, I thank You for those who are reading this book: history makers and flames. Plant them and root them in Your zealous heart for them. Let them feel Your pleasure as true revivalists.

About the Author

Roger Joyner is a leader in the Burn 24-7 and international house of prayer movement. He is a passionate leader in prayer and carries a heart for day and night worship and prayer to invade the earth. He currently lives in Oroville, California, with his wife, Gabrielle, and their two girls, Selah and Kinsey. They love to travel as a family and give encouragement to prayer and worship communities. You can contact Roger at www.rogerjoyner.com.

Chapter 12

God's Global March of Zeal

Sean Feucht

Not knowing what words to say, prayers to pray, or songs to sing in a meeting is not a common issue I encounter. It is not because I always know exactly what to say in every situation, but because I have intentionally integrated the principle of praying "without ceasing" (1 Thessalonians 5:17) as I travel around the world.

Even if I do not feel particularly "inspired" or "anointed" in a situation or meeting, there are always words, songs, and prayers that can be spoken, sung, and uttered. These are sometimes done so without the need for emotional feeling, yet banked upon "in faith." In my personal journey with the Lord, I have learned that consistency has been the key to walk in obedience to declare, sing, and prophesy repeatedly until the full manifestation of the promise comes to pass. Often I feel a greater pleasure of the Lord settle over my heart when I pray or sing in faith and feel nothing than when every sense in my body is tingling with the feeling of His nearness.

Yet it was an altogether different story this time around. I had nothing, and I mean absolutely nothing, to say. I stood speechless at the National Mall in downtown Washington D.C. I even stood a bit nervous. In just a matter of minutes, I was due to jump on stage in front of an enormous crowd to lead this diverse company in a siege of corporate prayer. The topic was specifically aimed at calling forth a youth revival and evangelistic mobilization in America greater than the days of the First and Second Great Awakening.

I have prayed prayers just like this in countless meetings, prayer rooms, youth rallies, and church services all over the world. This was not a new topic, and the very reason I was asked to lead intercession over this prayer target was because it burned in my heart and was the core of my calling.

This specific day had an even greater significance. Eight years earlier, as a seventeen-year-old junior in high school, I stood in virtually the same place with 450,000 from my generation. That day forever marked my life as I received a heavenly download of my calling to witness this dream come to pass. That single encounter changed everything in my life and led to this wild pilgrimage across the nations planting furnaces of worship and prayer to awaken the hearts of a generation.

But eight years later, something or maybe even Someone was blocking out every thought in my brain. It was like I was prohibited from regurgitating anything I had ever prayed or sung before.

My mind and heart was a blank canvas as I was called up to pray, and I was fully freaking out inside.

The Global March

All of the sudden, I was helplessly clinging to the promise of Jesus to "not worry about what you will say" as I stepped on the stage to face 50,000 worshippers (Mark 13:11). Here goes nothing! With a nervous heart and sweating palms, I grabbed the microphone and a strange confidence began to settle over me. A thought entered my mind that if I was obedient to just "open my mouth," maybe God would indeed "fill it" (Psalm 81:10).

Immediately, the Holy Spirit spoke two distinct things to my spirit on stage: "Isaiah 42" and "the march of zeal." Having no idea what verse, reference, or prayer this was, I opened my Bible as I introduced the prayer topic. While I was speaking, I thumbed to Isaiah 42, and this verse immediately jumped out at me—just in the nick of time!

> The LORD will march out like a mighty man, like a warrior he will stir up his zeal; with a shout he will raise the battle cry and will triumph over his enemies.
> —Isaiah 42:13, NIV

Not having remembered ever reading or meditating on this verse, I was instantly shocked at how much authority, triumph, and anointing were on these words. I remember wanting to re-read it over and over again for my own sake so it would sink in, but I thought that may be little awkward for some 50,000 onlookers.

I could hardly believe God purposely performed a full on "white out" of my mind right before this massive gathering while making my knees shake in the process! Then He totally bailed me out by dropping one of the greatest promises, hopes, and prophetic insights into heaven's mark of this global youth revival! As the sound waves from Isaiah were read and seemed to endlessly echo through the historic National Mall in America's capital city, the revelation of God's zeal emerged as the key component and catalyst of this move.

Zeal as a Man

In the same place where Martin Luther King's infamous "I have a dream" speech gripped a generation forty-five years earlier, these words from Isaiah suddenly became "active" and "alive" (Hebrews 4:12) in the company of such a great and historic assembly. As I was reading them, I had an experience unlike any time reading scripture publically before. I saw the words become a manifested reality in that moment. I watched Zeal march forth across America.

It was not zeal as a noun, a mere description or charismatic rhetoric. It was zeal as an actual Man! A screen opened above the praying crowd in that moment and the man Jesus, the very person of zeal, began marching forth from Washington D.C. all the way to San Francisco, California. He was armed with zeal, was releasing zeal, and was fully embodying zeal! Fierce, aggressive passion emitted as a contagion from His being in this march. Every place, person, and city He touched was forever changed. It was an inescapable virus and He was the emitting host.

I was undone in the moment while watching this holy infection envelop a generation like a hurricane slamming the East Coast of America. The widespread storm flushed away the norms of boredom, apathy, and immorality while depositing rising righteous zeal, passion, and holiness in its swath. The climate on the landscape forever changed.

This was an altogether new side of my Savior. I had never seen anything like this before in my journey with God. Just as Jesus sat down somewhere in between miracles, crusades, and revelatory teaching sessions to strategically and delicately weave bamboo strips into a fierce cord of whips, the disciples also had no grid for what was coming. They knew their beloved Rabbi as the compassionate healer, loving shepherd, and intimate friend. They witnessed the first-hand account of His kindness towards the woman with the issue of blood stretching out to touch His garment. They also spread the story of the extravagant mercy and tenderness extended to the adulterous woman during a dramatic showdown with the Pharisees. They understood, believed, and witnessed, "God is love," "God is mercy," and "God is kindness."

But they had yet to see Him display the wildness and aggression unleashed in the temple as He ferociously drove out the moneychangers on that unforgettable day. It was a completely new side of their Jesus unleashed. Upon beholding this scenario, Psalm 69:9 offered the only adequate language they quoted to describe what unfolded: "Zeal for your house consumes me" (John 2:17).

Zeal was being embodied, displayed, and released before their very eyes. The same "God is love" and "God is mercy" was also "God is zeal."

Zeal for His House

I'm sure the disciples, Pharisees, and moneychangers alike were shocked to see the Good Shepherd unleashing a torrent of emotional and physical vigor. They must have asked each other many questions while ducking their heads to avoid being stuck by the whip in His hand. "Why such an outburst and fanatical display? What would provoke Him like this? We've never seen

Him act like this before! What has so moved Him to be like a madman?"

His passion and zeal was aimed at destroying the perversion that had infested the house of the Lord. The motives of Jesus become clear when He declared: "My house will be called a house of prayer" (Matthew 21:13, NIV). Despite the rarity of such an occurrence in the Bible throughout the life and ministry of Jesus, it was not a mistake or any less "God-like" than the healings, compassion, and acts of kindness. This marking of zeal was fully who Jesus was, and nothing moved Him more than for God's house to be fully represented correctly. Jesus set a clear model for what all eager followers should display: an intense zeal for the house of the Lord.

Although you may not see nearly as many sermon series, book sales, or podcast downloads on the "Zeal of God" as you will the "Love of God," it does not make it any less important or crucial for our daily lives. It is still completely "God-like" and essential if we want to walk into the fullness of God's design for our lives.

The fact is that the reality of the "zeal of the Lord" does not always fit so perfectly into our God-in-our-image, consumer-driven, fluffy Christianity. The sad truth is that we do not understand the zeal of God and are therefore afraid of it. That is why preachers, scholars, and commentators alike shy away from the subject. It does not "sell" or is not as "palatable" as other attributes of God. Most likely this is because the zeal of God fully realized is the very thing that will shatter and rearrange our pretty, comfortable lives. It is probably because it is the very thing we need to hear, understand, and implement.

So how do we access and walk in this authentic zeal in our lives? How can we model what Jesus modeled in our daily lives?

You will not find the answer in a ten-step self-help book or by having the most zealous person you know lay hands on you in prayer. But this journey for zeal begins and ends with the quest for the likeness of God. For as we discovered in the life of Jesus, the likeness of God *is* true Zeal.

As we look in Isaiah 59:17 (NIV), we are again offered a glimpse into this inseparable attribute of the likeness of God:

> He put on righteousness as a breastplate, and the helmet of salvation on His head. He put on the garment of vengeance and wrapped himself in zeal as with a cloak.

As the image of the frantic swirl Jesus portrayed in the temple that day was forever emblazoned onto the hearts of His humble followers, this very truth is verified, validated, and prophesied first in the book of Isaiah. This insightful passage reveals that the very person of God is "wrapped in zeal." It is covers Him, shines forth from His being, and is all about Him. His entire being radiates with zealous fire and blazing passion!

Us Like Him

The first chapter in the Bible clearly describes that we were made in the very "likeness of God" (Genesis 1:27). We are the *Imago Dei* meaning "the image, shadow, and likeness of God." Unlike every other created thing and the earth itself, God formed man out of the dust, breathed into him, and bestowed upon him the most coveted thing in the universe—His very likeness.

The implications of this are absolutely staggering for every weak, tired, and overwhelmed human being when they crack open their eyes in the morning to face the challenges of a new day. We have the ability, calling, and ultimate potential to model the same characteristics that God embodies. This means we can actually think and look like God!

Just meditate for a moment on how this very foundational and biblical truth, when fully understood and implemented, could free a generation from the miry sludge of passivism, lethargy, and boredom! This simple revelation could break off all self-imposed limitations and lead us into inconceivable breakthrough.

Dubbed "new creations" from Romans 6:4, we have the privilege and invitation as born again believers to step into full-on God-likeness. When revelation dawns that we actually bear God's image, we are at once struck with the magnificence of our possibilities and the tragedy of our unrealized potential. Jesus authenticated hope for this by prophesying at the end of His ministry that His disciples would see "greater things" than even He performed (John 14:12). They did indeed see a manifestation in their day and we will also see them in ours.

With Jesus alone as our source of zeal, we can fully become what He is if we implement and manifest this reality in our lives. It's time for this prophetic word of emboldened zeal over a generation (from the vision in Washington D.C.) to manifest and become the "flesh" that "dwells among us" in this season of history (John 1).

Full of Godly Zeal

One of the most underrated and least-taught stories in the Bible has to be that of a man named Phinehas out of Numbers 25. It is surely one of the wildest and most theologically challenging stories testing the bedrock of every Christian's belief system. Steeped throughout this drama are key characteristics that reveal the depth of God's hatred toward wickedness and His generous reward ready for those who confront compromise with a zealous heart.

The precedent set through a young man's fiery zeal quelled God's plague against an entire nation and attracted a "covenant of lasting peace" extended to his entire lineage (verses 12–13). If there was ever a clear manifestation and biblical example of what walking in true zeal looks like, along with the benefits that accompany such a pursuit, the story of Phinehas is it.

As the grandson of the high priest Aaron, Phinehas was introduced onto a scene of widespread idolatry, sexual immorality, and obvious rebellion. Israelite men were breaking their sacred oaths with God and their families by bringing over idol-worshipping, foreign Moabite women into their cities and homes. These women carried wicked ways with them and filled the land with worship to Baal of Peor. They coerced the men of Israel to begin sacrificing and "bowing down" before false gods (verse 2). This was a movement of open and arrogant rebellion bringing down a nation slumped in apathy and tolerance. As these acts were even taking place in daylight before the people, the "Lord's anger burned against them" (verse 3).

Apathy, Tolerance, and Compromise

The wicked and rebellious acts of these men brought a disastrous plague upon the nation leaving over 24,000 dead as a result. In a desperate cry to end a heinous plague with a potential to wipe out the entire nation, the word of the Lord came to Moses and the judges to put to death in broad daylight any men who had joined in the worship to Baal of Peor. The line was now drawn in the sand and the command was given.

After the somber decree was issued, and while Moses, along with the entire nation, was repenting with tears before the Lord in front of the Tent of Meeting, something unimaginable took place. A man strolled in—in plain sight through this national repentance gathering—directly past Moses with a foreign Midianite woman at his side. This was an openly defiant move taking place on a day where multitudes were crying out for God's forgiveness in their sacred place of encounter (Tent of Meeting) to put an end to the widespread plague.

Imagine watching this take place! There must have been several double-takes and pinching of skin for anyone watching. What open desecration and adamant rebellion against God, Moses, and the entire nation! What blatant disrespect for the word of the Lord and the current structure of authority. What is possibly worse is that no watching this take place did anything about it in that moment, except one man.

While the leaders, judges, and multitude either chose to ignore this inconvenient scene or save the punishment for another day, one zealous, burning heart could not stand to watch another minute go by. Convenience alone could not hold him back. Righteousness had to shine forth and the zeal of the Lord alone could accomplish this. The miry sludge of compromise would not numb his conscience or extinguish the flame burning deep within.

Kill the Compromise

Upon beholding this site, Phinehas left the Tent of Meeting burning with holy anger. Grabbing his spear, he followed the man into his tent and drove the weapon into the man and woman killing them both on the spot. He did not politicize, delay, or calculate the risk of what would happen if this act were misunderstood. He could not hold back the fire of zeal burning within. In response to such a violent and immediate action, the plague against Israel was stopped (verse 8).

What a crazy story with an absolutely unbelievable ending! The entire fate of the nation rested on one PK's (pastor's kid's) ability to overcome the cultural tolerance and moral depravity that infiltrated the church of his day. Having grown up in church his entire life, it is almost assured that Phinehas witnessed the good, bad, and ugly of ministry and the church. Like so many, he could have easily used those experiences as an excuse to slide down the slippery slope of apathy, disillusionment, and compromise. Instead, he chose to face compromise head on and kill it.

This same untamable zeal drove teenage David to march into open battle exclaiming: "Who is this uncircumcised Philistine that he should defy the armies of the living God?" (1 Samuel 17:26) while flinging stones at a giant five times his size. It was the same flame inside that caused Jehu to "ride like a madman" while dismantling the perversion of Ahab and Jezebel shouting, "Come with me and see my zeal for the Lord!" to his enemies (2 Kings 10:16). It was the same passion that erupted inside Jesus creating a tumultuous tornado of righteous indignation to cleanse the temple from the "den of thieves" and restore it as a "house of prayer for all nations" (Mark 11:17). This is the zeal that raged inside Phineas to kill the sin and rid the land of compromise.

This same zeal is available to you today and to every hungry and humble heart postured to receive. These are but a few of the many biblical precedents to whet your appetite of how this can practically manifest in your life and change the world around you. However, these are examples of ordinary people who completely removed all areas of sin, compromise, and mixture in their lives.

This zeal of God will not co-exist within the confines of a life lived in compromise. It does not matter how many prayers you pray, songs you sing, books you read, or conferences you attend.

You cannot live a life of zeal based only upon the foundation of goose bumps you felt singing your favorite worship chorus at the altar. The true lasting zealous heart is forged in the fires of holiness possessing the will to "hate what is evil and cling to what is good" (Romans 12:9). This is the predecessor to the command, "Never be lacking in zeal, but keep your spiritual fervor" that is the very theme of this book. You cannot look, behave, and "wrap yourself in zeal" as God does until you love what He loves and hate what He hates. The implementation of zeal into our lives begins here: A quest for holiness.

Repentance and a Standard of Holiness

If you live in the place of compromise yet desire to see authentic zeal manifest in your life, there is only one option. You must take the spear of open repentance and drive it deep into the sin of compromise. Like with Phinehas, sometimes it requires an immediate, violent, and uncalculated response. Think of how fast the evil plagues over a generation would dissipate if every one of us responded like Phinehas. Dream of the standard of holiness and righteousness that could be raised if only for a few young brave souls that would dare pave the way!

> When the enemy comes in like a flood, the Spirit of the Lord will lift up a standard against him.
>
> —Isaiah 59:19, NKJV

You are the standard God is raising up in this hour. You are the very God-likeness wrapped in zeal and radiating holiness that an entire generation is longing to behold! You are the "sons of God" waiting to be revealed for which "all creation groans" (Romans 8:19).

It is time to courageously and immediately pick up the spear and run, run, run to kill every area of compromise that would hold you back from the fullness of your destiny in God! His zeal is longing to shine through a purified heart!

Rewards of Legacy

The most jaw-dropping facet of this story is not the actions of God to end the plague thus saving the entire nation (which is a pretty big deal), but rather His personal reward bestowed to Phinehas. This staggering response from God carries wild implications for every hungry heart on a journey to embody true zeal.

Below is what the Lord spoke to Moses concerning the actions of Phinehas:

> "Phinehas son of Eleazar, the son of Aaron, the priest, has turned my anger away from the Israelites for he was as zealous as I am for my honor among them, so that in my zeal I did not put an end to them. Therefore tell him I am making my covenant of peace with him. He and his descendants will have a covenant of lasting priesthood, because he was zealous for the honor of his God and made atonement for the Israelites."
>
> —Numbers 25:10–13, NIV

There are some life and legacy-altering statements made here by the Lord concerning Phinehas. The first of these being that this grandson of Aaron was "as zealous as I am for my honor." What an incredible statement to be made! This is the first time in human history where the Lord declared that a man actually carried the same measure of zeal that He Himself carries. Can you now imagine the potential created by this precedent for each of us on this journey together? This statement declares that it is in fact possible to posses a God-like zeal and passion! I can almost hear the cheering by the hosts in heaven as this wave of revelation now crashes on the shores of our hearts!

The second staggering remark is how this one holy action could cause God to bless not just the life of Phinehas but also the entire lineage to come after him. An ordinary man acted in courageous and righteous obedience to God and forever made his mark on history. What a legacy to leave your family name! Proverbs 13:22 declares that "a wise man leaves an inheritance for his children's children." Just mediate on the reality that such a violent act warranted a "covenant of peace" from God for his children's children's children! Phinehas exerted holy rage against sin so that his lineage could live in absolute peace. What a heritage! We can therefore agree that acts of zeal reverberate in the heart of God throughout generations.

Zeal: the Life Saver

The concepts, teachings, history, and revelations on the subject of zeal in this book are but the beginning as to what is available for seeking hearts. Virtually every story in the Bible, move of God throughout history, and notable revivalist has been known and marked by this God-like attribute. The "fleshing out" of these words, stories, and embodiment of zeal in our daily lives is essential to see this become more than ink on a page. Godly zeal MUST become reality in our generation. It must manifest on the earth. From journeys across the frontiers of unreached nations, to the faithfulness of our nine-to-five jobs in the workplace, to the mundane tasks of daily life, heaven has an endless reservoir of zeal and passion stored up for us to draw from!

As I conclude this chapter and this book, I'd like to share how zeal manifested itself in my own life at a time and place I least expected it. Here is a story of zeal that forever changed my life.

It actually saved my life.

A few years ago I was in the sprawling Ugandan capital of Kampala. I was utterly weary and downright delusional after traveling for thirty-six hours by bus through the East African nations of Burundi, Rwanda, and Uganda. It was disgustingly hot, dusty, and the non-air-conditioned bus ride from Bujumbura to Kampala was littered with border delays, winding mountain roads, car wrecks, and classic, perpetual African interruptions. It seems nothing goes smoothly or as planned on this side of the planet.

After our twelve-hour-late arrival at our destination, my Ugandan friend and I rode in three separate taxis for two hours to get from the bus station to the house where we stayed a few villages away. This would give us just about four hours of sleep before my flight departed the next morning to the USA via Europe.

Riding on a spiritual high from the previous two weeks of incredible breakthrough across the region, we were still celebrating God's faithfulness in our current state of physical exhaustion. It was one of those moments like Paul stated where we didn't know if we were in or out of the body (2 Corinthians 12:3), but we were sure happy and joy-filled! With our own eyes, we had witnessed terminal diseases healed, Muslims and Hindus radically saved, countless hearts ignited, and worship and prayer communities birthed. It was a trip of a lifetime!

As we were bringing the last load of luggage from the taxi into the house, three men shoved us through the door while driving the butt of their AK-47 assault rifles into our backs. They threw us to the ground and began yelling in a Swahili tongue, demanding from us money, passports, and any valuables. As they repeatedly kicked and beat us, the barrel of their loaded gun was pressed against our skulls, grinding our faces into the hard cement floor.

Having followed us since we first got off the bus hours before, they claimed they were going to "rob, torture, and kill the American." Knowing the crime-infested terrain of East Africa, almost all thieves kill their victims so they cannot be identified after their crime.

I felt like this could be the end as moments from the previous year flooded my mind and heart. The fact that we did not have much money (as it was the end of the trip) and they could not find my passport (hidden in a secret pocket) was making them more agitated as they continued to breathe threats against us while scattering our belongings across the house.

As they continued to pillage through our luggage, they discovered numerous Bibles and overtly Christian books. This caused them to scream to their subdued captors lying on the ground: "Are you followers of The Way?"

Here we go. This was the scenario and the very question that we felt might never happen to us. Yet it is the very question running through every believer's mind as we contemplate our personal loyalty to Jesus. Would we stand up in defiant courage and face death for our Savior? Or would we cowardly shrink back and deny Him? This was my question. This was my test. This was my reality in that moment.

Something took place on the inside of my spirit that I cannot explain. The implications of my answer bypassed the critical thinking of my mind and the inner roaring zeal of my heart exploded with an emphatic answer: "YES! I am a follower of Jesus! YES!" Two times again they demanded an answer to the same question. Two times I responded with the same rumble. Silence then fell upon the room. As I waited for the response of the detonation of a bullet down the barrel of that gun, the flood of zeal now released could not be stopped.

It was as if the gates of the dam holding back passion broke open and praise, worship, and my prayer language exuded forth like a river! The stewardship of my inner and personal zeal and love for Jesus instantly manifested in the scariest moment of my life. We all began worshipping, praying, and boisterously lifting our prayer language to heaven. As we were caught up in worship and the Presence of God filled the room, we hardly noticed that our armed captors had slipped out of the room and vanished!

Whether these thieves saw giant angels standing our midst, became threatened in that moment, or were simply freaked out at our boisterous response, I firmly believe that zeal and passion saved our lives that day.

Join the March of Zeal

What you steward in the secret places of your life will always manifest in the public places. The world is longing for the "marching out of zeal" (Isaiah 42:13) in our neighborhoods, communities, schools, workplaces, and mission frontiers around the world. It is time for us to embody what we believe and so boldly proclaim. It is time to manifest this reality on the earth. The time for an authentic move of zeal is now.

Will you join this global march? Will you call forth the full and immediate manifestation of that holy passion lying dormant inside your heart? I promise you it is there. He is there. In this very moment, this very simple prayer of consecration could change the course of your life. I don't believe that you picked up this book only to hear a few inspiring stories and move on with your life. You have this book for a reason. This is your moment.

For a generation drowning in the ocean of apathy, tolerance, and compromise, Christ in *you* is the hope of glory for this world! Can you hear the mundane workplace environments, university campuses, and third-world mission fields begging for a revelation of the true children of God Paul spoke of in Romans 8:19? These are those who are clearly "not of this world," neither are they weighed down with the preoccupations of this world. They are "sons of light, daughters of the day" and fully expect to see the kingdom of God manifest everywhere their feet tread. Compromise, timidity, and fear have bowed their knee to the supremacy of the King of zeal reigning in their lives! Who wants in?

Saying YES will bring a holy confrontation to every area not dominated by the righteous zeal of God in your life. By wholeheartedly agreeing, engaging, and praying aloud this simple prayer from sincerity, your life will forever be marked. It is as if you are giving Jesus the green light to enter your heart and rid your "temple" of compromise, complacency, and cowardice, and then fill it with His glory. He is a zealous God of love and passion jealous for our all.

Pray this prayer out loud with me:

> God, I come before You with great expectation in heart and hunger in my spirit! I want so much more of You than ever before! I give You all of me in this moment once again. I want to be consumed in Your burning and zealous eyes and become that which I behold! Pour out Your grace on me now to clear away all clutter in my life and clearly see the call of zeal. Show me how to establish this as the foundation of

my life! From this moment onwards, I choose to leave behind all apathy, compromise, and passivity in my life! I destroy any amount of hesitation, pessimism, and cynicism that has found its root in the soil of my heart! I break all alliances and remove all hindrances that would put a ceiling on the explosion of zeal You want to awaken in my life!

I diligently commit myself to apprehend the truths set forth in Your Word! I want to embody a zeal that lasts beyond the pages of this book and the momentary stirring I even feel in this moment! I desire to live in a multi-generational impartation of zeal that extends well beyond my eighties and passes down as inheritance to my children's children! I choose to make the mundane moments of my life dry kindling for Your fresh fire! Invade every area of my personal and public space and do what only You can do! Make this simple prayer a manifest reality in this season. I surrender to Your will and give You my life.

Amen.

About the Author

Sean Feucht is a husband, father, lover, fighter, optimist, musician, speaker, writer, revivalist, and founder of a grassroots global worship, prayer, and missions organization called Burn 24/7. His lifelong quest and dream is to witness a generation of burning hearts arise across the nations of the world with renewed faith, vision, and sacrificial pursuit after the Presence of God with reckless abandon. He has produced, recorded, and released twelve worship albums, numerous teaching resources, and recently coauthored his first book *Fire and Fragrance*. He is married to his gorgeous wife, Kate, and is a father to their two children: Keturah Liv and Malachi Christopher. He currently resides in Harrisburg, Pennsylvania (when he is not on planes, trains, or automobiles). Contact Sean at www.seanfeucht.com or www.burn24-7.com.

Endnotes

1   Danny Silk, *Dream Life*, audio teaching, (Redding: Bethel Church, 2009).

2   Liam De Paor (translation and commentaries), *Saint Patrick's World: The Christian Culture of Ireland's Apostolic Age,* (Notre Dame, Indiana: University of Notre Dame Press, 1993), 100.

3   Lindy Conant, "Every Nation, Every Soul," www.lindyconant.com, Used by permission.

4   Elizabeth Barrett Browning, *Aurora Leigh*, ed. editor Kerry Sweeney (Oxford: Oxford University Press, 1993), 246.

5   Lou Engle and Catherine Paine, *Fast Forward: A Call to Millennial Prayer Revolution* (Pasadena: Wells of Revival, 1999).

Authored by
Sean Feucht & Andy Byrd

Available in the Store at
www.seanfeucht.com

www.fireandfragrance.com

www.thecircuitrider.com

www.burn24-7.com